Eric R. Severson

Scandalous Obligation

RETHINKING
CHRISTIAN
RESPONSIBILITY

BEACON HILL PRESS
OF KANSAS CITY

ISBN 978-0-8341-2612-1

Printed in the
United States of America

Cover Design: Doug Bennett
Interior Design: Sharon Page

Library of Congress Cataloging-in-Publication Data

Severson, Eric. R.
    Scandalous obligation : rethinking Christian responsibility / Eric Severson.
        p. cm.
    Includes bibliographical references.
    ISBN 978-0-8341-2612-1 (pbk.)
    1. Responsibility. 2. Christian ethics. I. Title.
    BJ1245.S48 2011
    241—dc22

                                                        2011006291

10 9 8 7 6 5 4 3 2 1

DEDICATION

For Bob and Karen Severson, who opened me to the mystery of Christian responsibility

CONTENTS

PREFACE

Books are dangerous. Among many other dangers, books fall from the printing press without an author to stand alongside the reading. The words are left to stand on their own virtues. No amount of illustrations, charts, or online forums can alleviate this danger. This particular book was written alongside colleagues and friends, many of whom were my students, who could ask questions of its author at any moment. Most readers of this volume will not have such a luxury. Thus it is critical that this book have a preface to quite literally stand before the face of these chapters.

First and foremost, this book is meant as a mirror for self-examination and not as a magnifying glass for scrutinizing others.[1] The words about responsibility here are meant to guide readers into considering the reach and extent of responsibility. Readers may be tempted to use notions of responsibility here in the accusatory, to define how other people have been responsible or irresponsible. The goal of the text, however, is to stimulate self-reflection and to generate conversations about the scope and reach of Christian responsibility. The core question at stake here is this: "When am I responsible?" Plenty of people are eager to write books about the irresponsibility of others or calling other people to responsibility. This book is more personal and thus perhaps more threatening.

Scandalous Obligation asks readers to consider the possibility that the concept of responsibility has often been overlooked, misunderstood, and shortchanged. This investigation proceeds by asking many questions about the way responsibility is dealt with in the Bible and in everyday life. The questions raised here are seldom answered directly. Readers may be uncomfortable that this book is decidedly more interested in asking questions than in providing answers. There is reasoning behind this sometimes-maddening strategy. When it comes to matters of Christian obligation, easy answers immediately run the risk of legalism and thus create loopholes that serve to justify the evasion of responsibility.

There is another danger with this book that needs to be addressed in preface to the chapters ahead. *Scandalous Obligation* will certainly suggest that humans are deeply responsible and called to take responsibility for the cloud of suffering that hangs over this world. By destabilizing the lines and limits on responsibility, this book runs a severe risk of piling guilt on the heads of people who already have been made to feel supremely guilty. The concept of guilt is tricky; it refers to a psychological state, a legal determination, and a moral situation. This book is not about feeling guilty but about exploring the ways in which the Christian self is bound to the suffering of the other.

Fyodor Dostoyevsky wrote, through one of his characters in *The Brothers Karamazov*, "All I know is that there is suffering and none are guilty."[2] In attempting to awaken the reader to a responsibility that embraces the suffering of the world, this book risks overwhelming people who are already acutely aware of guilt and responsibility. The idea that responsibility might require even more than what already overwhelms us may be cause for unrelenting despair.

By pushing obligation into the realm of the scandalous, this book takes this very risk. Why not despair if responsibility is so deep and perilous? This scandal can, and perhaps should, be a cause for despair. Yet as Søren Kierkegaard teaches us, Christians know more than one sort of despair.[3] There is, of course, despair that looks like depression and strips away any hope of joy, comfort, or peace. Despair of this sort is perhaps inevitable if responsibility is about being good enough. Has not Christianity struggled for centuries with the question of human goodness and the capacity of communities and individuals to be good? Augustine's famous disagreement with Pelagius hinges on this very issue. Perhaps it is already Cain's problem in the book of Genesis; he is maddened by his own incapacity to present an adequate sacrifice.[4] It seems rather critical that Christians know another kind of despair, a despair that leads to life. This is a saving despair, an abandoning of any hope of ever being good enough or ever being completely and resoundingly responsible. I hope this book points toward this second kind of despair, a despair that will hopefully make vivid the need for grace and the need for a dedication to justice that is not shaken by the depth and breadth of responsibility.

There is a third kind of despair mentioned by Kierkegaard. He points out that perhaps the most frightening form of despair is the kind we are not aware we have. This problem is a sharp one when it comes to any quest to understanding responsibility. It is perilous, after all, to carry around a sickness without any awareness of the ailment. Sometimes when I am coming down with a cold or the flu I try to ignore the symptoms or pretend they are due to allergies or fatigue. Likewise, this third type of despair shows up occasionally, in glimpses, but I quickly grow adept at explaining away the unsettling appearance of such anxieties. When it comes to responsibility, it is alarmingly easy to develop the skills to pretend I am immune to the quiet call to attend to the suffering of the other person. In such a mode, I turn quickly away from those corners of the world and those parts of the Bible that call into question the stability of the fragile fiction I have spun to convince myself I am a responsible person. If Christian obligation is scandalous, as I wish to argue here, the Bible will be found to repeatedly shame this inclination to shield my eyes from the scandal.

This book is not for everyone. It takes a certain degree of courage to challenge the lines and boundaries of responsibility that we have assumed and relied on for a lifetime. This short book is relentless in questioning the limits that Christians tend to place on responsibility. Readers who do not wish to reconsider their assessment of Christian responsibility have picked up the wrong book and should put it down immediately.

There are routine and essential references to the Bible in the pages that follow. The Bible is not invoked to close down questions or finalize investigations. Rather, I suspect that a deeper understanding of responsibility must involve a reconsideration of the scandalous texts that have been too often tamed by contemporary moral visions. The ancient themes of the Bible, I will argue, are more than just knickknacks or vestiges of a bygone era. The call to responsibility in Jewish and Christian scripture is surprising and offensive, particularly to people who have grown accustomed to a more reasonable approach to obligation. My suspicion throughout this book is that genuine Christian responsibility exceeds and eclipses the domesticated version that so often passes for moral obligation. My argument is that the sacred texts of Judaism and Christianity announce a new way to be responsible.

I do not, even for an instant, suppose that I write this book as one who has grasped or understood the depths and dynamics of Christian responsibility. Instead I write as one who has become painfully aware of my own despair, shaken from my ignorance by suffering faces and by scriptural passages. Biblical responsibility sometimes seems unreasonable, even scandalous, but the tendency is to ignore this scandal and pretend these symptoms do not indicate a deeper illness. If this book is unrelenting, may it point in unrelenting fervor toward the embrace of a sickness that leads to grace and life.

ACKNOWLEDGMENTS

This book is, more than I even realize, the product of a community. Many dedicated students, colleagues, and friends at Eastern Nazarene College have helped to shape and reshape each chapter.

I wish to thank several readers whose thoughts and conversations directly influenced the content of this book, including Patrick Pasik, Kurtis Biggs, Ashley Jardim, Karen Marshall, Joel Paulson, Karl Giberson, Luke Cochran, Jay Wilson, Christina Gschwandtner, Emily Michelle Ledder, and many others. I also appreciate the support offered by Eastern Nazarene College for the writing of this book.

This book owes a great deal of philosophical debt to the work of Emmanuel Levinas, whose discussions of responsibility and holiness have influenced more of the ideas in this book than citation can properly credit.

I am grateful to my parents, whose commitment to Christian responsibility has always inspired me. To my children, Marie, Ty, and Luke, who make occasional appearances in these pages, I offer gratitude that I hope they grow to understand. Finally, I thank my wife, Misha, who has no idea how thoroughly she has impacted the pages of this book.

one

RESPONSIBILITY RECONSIDERED

A SNOWBALL whizzed past my ear, planting itself on a nearby tree. I stood paralyzed for a moment, arms full of books and papers. To stand motionless was surely to be hit. Prudence might compel me to run quickly for cover. But I've never been one to pass up the opportunity to throw a few snowballs. After about five minutes of hand-numbing fun, I gathered my soaked papers off the snow and headed into a campus building, leaving students behind me to continue the fight without my help. After about ten minutes in the building I returned to that same doorway to find several shamefaced undergraduates staring mournfully at a broken window. To their credit, they had not fled the scene. They were not quite sure what to do; one of them jokingly blamed me for the broken glass.

I praised them for their honesty, patted them on the backs, and went back to my duties as professor at a small Christian college. My window happens to overlook the field and the carnage, and as I tried to craft a lecture on responsibility, I couldn't help but ponder that fuzzy line where responsibility begins and ends. How responsible was I for that broken window? The question seems rather simple and straightforward. In a court of law I would almost certainly be exonerated. I hadn't thrown the offending missile, and the window at the center of the controversy had been intact when I entered the building. No discernable cause-and-effect process tied me directly to the crime, nor would a reasonable person accuse me of being "to blame" for the event. I had been a part of the melee, and it was unclear who had thrown the errant snowball, but both my lack of arm strength and absence from the scene during the crime seemed to release me from any sort of responsibility. Still, does the fact that I was not tied to the crime by fault truly relieve me of responsibility?

Instincts, honed since childhood, drive us to find our way out of responsibilities when they can be avoided. Responsibility comes with hassle, cost, pain, and risk. We give people credit for being "good" when they own up to their tangible and obvious duties. The term "charity" tends to designate unprovoked, voluntary donations of time, money, or goods. We drop money into Salvation Army buckets at Christmas and occasionally donate to fight hunger or cancer. But even in these cases we tend to think of the sacrifice as charity and not responsibility. The term "responsibility" is reserved for situations in which people are legally or morally obliged to assist. This tendency is reinforced by ages of cultural, legal, and even religious support. At face value, responsibility seems to be determined by way of blame. We only find ourselves responsible for others when we can be connected legally to their suffering.

It is that concept, responsibility, so widely and diversely understood, which serves as the focal point for this book. This journey is driven by a suspicion that the concept of responsibility needs to be rethought on broad and practical levels. We will explore a host of ways in which responsibility is shifted, shirked, passed, and ignored. The core questions here relate to the posture with which humans ought to encounter strangers, enemies, the poor, and the oppressed. This is thus a book about social justice, about the questions that arise when humans, and Christians in particular, analyze the length and breadth of their responsibility for a broken world.

The concept of responsibility appears all over the world today. When something goes wrong, we want to know who is responsible. Journalists scramble to be the first to identify the culprit behind the suffering splashed on our screens and newspapers. Whether investigating disasters like 9/11, Hurricane Katrina, or the 2007 Virginia Tech University shooting, the world wants to know *who* is responsible.

Children learn at a shockingly early age how to sidestep or embrace responsibility for broken windows and blackened eyes. "Responsibility" is a word wielded effectively by governments, who encourage citizens to do their "civic duty." Charities implore us to take responsibility for the poor, the wounded, the oppressed, and the overlooked. Religion, in its nearly infinite manifestations, often challenges humans to carefully consider a kind of supreme and transcendent responsibility.

One does not have to look far to see a host of conflicting models offered through various political, theological, and ethical perspectives. The variety of attitudes toward responsibility doesn't hide in dusty ethical textbooks. They make themselves known in the games we play, the media that enchants us, and certainly in the myriad of cultural traditions that inform daily life. Ethics, the philosophy of responsibility, is everywhere. This book is driven by the sense that there is something profoundly wrong with the way responsibility is developed in the world today. Some of the problems I am eager to identify may be peculiar to my corner of the human experience. Some of them pertain to global problems, some to North American problems, and there is always that chance that some of them only pertain to me. Still, the concept of responsibility seems sufficiently broken to warrant a close look and a careful examination.

Responsibility is inherently practical. A philosophy of obligation that does not translate into tangible human behavior is a silly contradiction. The explorations of this book make use of resources ranging from television and art to ethical philosophy. With these tools we will seek a fresh perspective on responsibility as it is lived and ignored in modern society. We will explore a variety of themes from religious and philosophical traditions around the world and across history. I am wagering, from the outset, that the Jewish and Christian traditions call for a form of responsibility that is easily overwhelmed, tainted, and obscured by the louder and more visible models that drive our daily interactions. Our discussions here will gradually push for a close association between the Christian gospel and concern for "the least of these" (see Matt. 25).

My hope for this book is that readers will join me in searching for the humble way responsible human communities should meet strangers, foreigners, neighbors, widows, and orphans. The philosophies of responsibility offered by popular media and politics simply cannot answer the call for justice that rises, sometimes silently, from the faces of those who suffer.

In religion, the question of responsibility has too often been reduced to a game whose goal is to figure out how to secure divine approval. In such a contest one's neighbor becomes profoundly secondary to the concept of obligation. The whole pursuit of responsibility is oriented toward the self. Inside and outside of religion, the question of responsibility has repeatedly returned to the self, the "I." Responsibility has come to refer to the extent to which a person must meet obligations to other people in order to fulfill the requirements of "goodness." Perhaps this echoes the young man, often called the rich young ruler, who approached Jesus to ask, "What must I do to inherit eternal life?" (Mark 10:17). The question is already loaded with a self-centered perspective on responsibility. The young man stumbled his way to Jesus in search of his own salvation, in search of his own eternal bliss. The problem he longed to solve was his own insecurity, his own doubts and fears about his spiritual status. This young man, sincere as he might be, already had his opinions about responsibility. He came to Jesus to discover the key to winning the game he was already playing.

Told to give all he had to the poor and to come follow Jesus, the young man became discouraged and overwhelmed. He walked away, kicking the dust. His disappointment may stem less from the extreme nature of Jesus' requirements than from his broken model of responsibility. Jesus asked him to be *more* responsible than can be considered reasonable. This result often jars modern readers. Hearing this story we imagine selling our houses and cars, dropping off bags of cash at homeless shelters, and setting out to live as vagrant wanderers. But these images miss the point as clearly as the young ruler himself. Jesus is offering a different model of responsibility, a different way to think of poverty and suffering and holiness. The old model, the young man's game, seems to be a pretty common one in the world today. People tend to ask the question of responsibility for self-centered reasons. What might it mean to ask the question of responsibility for the sake of others? For the sake of the poor?

The young ruler and the modern reader of that narrative look in vain for a measure against which they can judge their worthiness. The measure is not offered by Jesus, except in an absurd gesture toward a bottomless responsibility that would leave the follower broken, totally given over to the poor and to the ministry of Jesus. Jesus has not tweaked the ruler's model for responsibility but offered an overwhelming alternate model. This book does not offer any definitive answers about how this new model should function but sets out on a journey toward the kind of responsibility that somehow exceeds the question, "What *must* I do?"

Human communities tend to ascribe responsibility where fault is found. At best, we are to take responsibility for the suffering in the world we have caused. Sadly there is a host of suffering in the world for which no one claims responsibility, either because of negligence or because there are truly no identifiably guilty parties. In many cases the guiltiest parties are ignorant of the damages they cause, far from the suffering, or even long dead. Modern racism and sexism sometimes operate this way, as contemporary societies reap the whirlwind of past sins. To make matters worse, the habits of culture and history make us blind to the ways we reproduce and reenact the injustices of our ancestors. Responsibility cannot be simply tied to the damages we cause, as our judges and juries are encouraged to assess. Such a perspective on responsibility, pivotal in proving fault in courts of law, is hopelessly ill-equipped to deal with the suffering that abounds in the world today.

Our courts are often at a loss when it comes to allocating responsibility. In 2006 a New York man stumbled out of a bar after watching a hockey game in Manhattan. Drunk and clumsy, he fell onto the subway tracks and was badly injured by a downtown train. The driver of the train, for his part, mistook the drunken man on the tracks for an "inert object." Struggling to place blame in the right place, the courts found the injured man "35 percent" responsible for his own injuries; his settlement was therefore reduced by that amount.[1] This game reduces responsibility to a formula. But this is a sad calculus, full of equations that will never balance out.

The problems of social justice are bolstered by a more fundamental quandary in interpersonal morality. When I encounter another person, I come face-to-face with someone whose needs, history, scars, fears, hopes, and dreams far exceed my comprehension. The other person needs more than I can give, hurts more than I can see, has been through more than I can understand, and hopes more that I can imagine. In this sense, the other person passes above and beyond my understanding. How can I be responsible for all these overwhelming, untraceable, and even unknown issues? Should we be considered responsible for what we cannot know or understand? Our journey moves toward an understanding of responsibility appropriate for a world overflowing with injustice. But this investigation must confront the unsettling fact that our duties are not particularly well defined. How responsible am I for the unknown and infinite needs and hurts that exceed my knowledge and abilities? Among the tensions that will constantly haunt this book is the paralysis that can be produced by competing responsibilities. When we choose, after all, which charity we will support, we are less vocally denouncing and refusing most of the others. When we choose an intimate friendship with one person, we are declining others this access to our lives. When we choose one career, we denounce most others, at least for a time. People regularly choose to live irresponsibly, squandering life and resources on selfish and shortsighted choices. But even when we attempt to be responsible, we remain caught between competing claims on how we ought to act. Pay attention at election time; candidates from every political party will beg you to come to the poll and vote "responsibly." This tension is seldom acknowledged, dwelling often as a subtle uneasiness that plagues us even as we overcome the temptation to live selfishly and resolve to make responsible choices. This lack of *ease*, sometimes called *dis*-ease, stands squarely in our way as we attempt to live responsibly.

Some of the most polarizing and fascinating ethical tensions in contemporary society reveal this tension. Pressed to rectify and prevent the injustices of racial and gender discrimination, we are faced with a difficult choice. Should companies hire and schools admit students with lower qualifications based on the gender or ethnicity of the applicant? Affirmative action is a complex and divisive issue, precisely because it appeals to a double responsibility. We feel responsible to hardworking candidates with the strongest SAT scores and sturdiest résumés. Simultaneously, we would be negligent to suppose that social and economic pressures fail to influence scores, grades, and personal histories. It is understandable that people weigh in passionately both in favor and opposition to affirmative action. On our best days, we establish opinions on ethical issues, not because our positions serve our own interests, but because we deem our stances maximally just. We hope that our efforts and opinions lead to a better, fairer world for everyone involved. Some issues, including affirmative action, place us in a tension that refuses to be easily resolved. We are pressed by authentic requests for responsibility on multiple sides. The temptation, to be sure, is to scoff at one request for justice and sleep easily at night.

The tension of competing responsibilities illustrated by affirmative action is the tip of the iceberg. Pressed to live frugally so we might direct resources to the poor, we buy clothing sewn by children in a South American sweatshop. Longing to avoid wastefulness we readily donate our used clothing to charities, flooding the world's clothing market with cast-off American clothing. Struggling to live responsibly with our ecological environment, we pour enough money into a hybrid Toyota Prius to inoculate a small country against the tetanus virus.[2] Tensions like these fill our daily lives with a sense of absurdity and with the very real danger of hypocrisy. Moral "high ground" is harder to achieve than we would like to think. This reality does not, of course, make the struggle any less vital.

We should also be painfully aware of the temptation to treat these pressing disagreements as a game. Savvy students often identify the irresolvable tensions inherent to problems like affirmative action, global poverty, and environmental degradation. In these issues, and in countless others, trying to rectify an unjust situation runs the risk of worsening the injustice or wasting energy on frivolous initiatives. There is a strange brand of comfort afforded by cynicism, which justifies inaction by identifying the potential perils of every action. This may be one of the more dangerous perils awaiting anyone who enters the complex and messy field of applied ethics. Cynical critiques come easy, far easier than pursuing solutions for the painful issues that plague our world.

We struggle with and against a seemingly natural impulse to draw a very tight line around our area of responsibility. Guilt, a sensation most people wish to avoid, is often tied directly to responsibility. We feel guiltiest when we see suffering that can be tied directly to our actions. So when we can show ourselves and others that we are not responsible for suffering, we directly address the way guilt influences our lives. Courts, juries, and judges provide one way of addressing the question of responsibility. Phrases like "probable cause" and "beyond reasonable doubt" are meant to establish the likelihood that an accused person can be connected to a crime. To avoid a guilty verdict, defendants seek to dissociate themselves from the cause-and-effect process by which someone or something was harmed. Tobacco companies blame consumers for abusing their products; countless murderers have blamed their crimes on temporary bouts of insanity; jilted lovers blame their enraged behavior on their unfaithful spouses. To find a person "guilty" in court prosecutors must usually establish either intentional wrongdoing or negligence. The defendant must be shown to act either maliciously or with a gross lack of ordinary concern for others. For the most part, acquittals rest on undermining the causal link between the accused and the crime. "If it doesn't fit, you must acquit."[3]

Even more sinister is the question of intentionality. We excuse ourselves from responsibility, consciously or otherwise, when we feel as though we "did not mean to do it." But the world is full of broken windows nobody meant to break. Human society is rife with corrupt systems nobody intended to distort. This is not to insinuate that we have any shortage of intentional acts of greed, selfishness, and abuse. These abound, to be sure. But what concerns me here is my own ability to acquit myself of responsibility for broken windows and scarred bodies. Nobody likes to feel complicit for the suffering of others; but to what lengths do we go to avoid the pang of a guilty conscience? For these reasons, responsibility is often reduced to what can be pinned on people.

I was eager to pay for the window broken in the snowball fight, despite my lack of direct fault in the breaking. But what concerns me is that I viewed my act as charity, not as responsibility. In this instance, charity allowed me to stand morally distinct from the seemingly careless behavior of my students. My act was still about me and my desire to be charitable. Even when I act generously to rectify injustice, I long for my actions to be seen as charity, not compulsory behavior based on unavoidable responsibility that has fallen to me. But perhaps the quotable actor Peter Ustinov had it right when he quipped, "It is our responsibilities, not ourselves, that we should take seriously."[4]

This book will traverse a broad cross section of fields and topics. One cannot attempt to explore the concept of responsibility without engaging, among many other disciplines, anthropology, psychology, sociology, politics, philosophy, and religion. The lines between these fields are sometimes blurry, sometimes distinct, but the primary orientation of the book is ethical. It must be underscored from the outset that I do not write as one who has discovered the answers to the ethical issues engaged here. It is critical, of course, to seek solutions to the ethical challenges that plague human existence. So this book is riddled with suggestions about how we might make such judgments and live differently because of them. Ethics, after all, is truly useless if it does not lead to actions and decisions. Still, this book is primarily intended to encourage readers to thoroughly consider the deceptively complex concept of responsibility and think through the implications of everyday claims about personhood, otherness, justice, and love.

Above all, this is a book about responsible engagement of the world. These reflections presume a reader who is interested in thinking about responsibility beyond the bounds of what can be proven in court, or required by any prescriptive code. This book is for communities and individuals who long to *take responsibility* for the broken bodies, empty plates, and leaking roofs of the world, even without a causal link binding them to the injustice. We must also learn to *act* on behalf of this suffering, despite the confusion that arises when we are less than sure which remedy we should seek.

Ironically, responsibility may sometimes require *inaction*, for not every act of compassion is actually helpful or beneficial to people caught in the vice of suffering and oppression. In the past fifty years, more than one trillion dollars in development-related foreign aid has been channeled from rich countries to various countries in Africa. Unfortunately, this well-intentioned generosity has frequently strengthened the political and economic problems behind hunger and disease in Africa. This doesn't mean that richer countries should ignore suffering in Africa or be released from responsibility for African suffering. Yet it certainly means that taking responsibility for suffering on that continent is more complicated than writing checks and dropping pallets of food from airplanes.

We must remain mindful; taking responsibility is not always about *doing* more.

Responsibility is much more than the duties reluctantly pinned on people who fail to acquit themselves of blame. The concept of responsibility, as it will be presented here, is about awakening to the sense that I *am* my responsibility. My very identity is bound up in responsibilities I have not chosen or sought. Responsibility isn't something I can take or leave. Children awaken to a world in which they are already responsible, already bound to others. Unfortunately, negative and legal notions of obligations have hijacked the concept of responsibility. This leaves me only responsible for the direct results of my intentional actions. Responsibility as blame distorts the very heart of humanity, let alone Christianity. To be human is to be responsible, to be bound both wonderfully and frighteningly to the faces that surround us.

This is not another book encouraging readers to be charitable, though love and charity are certainly pivotal to what follows. But neither blame nor charity provides an adequate tool for understanding responsibility. This is a book about the slippery nature of obligation, the competing calls to justice, and the perilous temptation to dismiss and avoid responsibility. This is a book about faces unattached to causes, suffering that never hits front pages or bumper stickers. Our journey takes us to the heart of a world full of gaping needs that hide no romance, charm, or glory. This is a book about an overlooked concept of the utmost importance for human life and community. This is a book about justice, about reconciliation, and about hospitality. In a word, this book is an invitation to reconsider the very notion of responsibility.

two

INVISIBLE CRIME

OF ALL the magical powers and abilities that inhabit the worlds of fantasy and fiction, which is the most desirable? The question has been used to pass countless hours of study hall, bus rides, and lazy summer days. The power to fly? X-ray vision? Tremendous strength? Spidey sense? Among the leading contenders is the power of invisibility, a fascination that traces back thousands of years. There is something intriguing about the power to interact with the world undetectably. Our fascination with invisibility is reflected back to us in movies like *Hollow Man* and *The Lord of the Rings*. The power to become undetectable totally alters the way one responds to the world. For Kevin Bacon's terrifying character in *Hollow Man*, every shady personality trait becomes magnified when he becomes invisible. Something strange happens when he no longer stands face-to-face with the people who are influenced by his actions. In *The Lord of the Rings* the theme is more nuanced. No character can handle the ring's power of invisibility completely, though some manage better than others. The ring's allure is to *see* without being *seen* and therefore to act without consequence. Fictional persons find themselves liberated from the arresting, restraining gaze of another face. And in this freedom they find an unparalleled rush. This fantasy has been repeated in many different tales, from Harry Potter's invisibility cloak to the classic novel *The Invisible Man*.

The idea of invisibility presents an important moral question, and a very old one: "Would you remain morally upstanding if no one was watching?" Plato reflected on this question at length, invoking a familiar story from Greek mythology.[1] Gyges was a lowly shepherd pasturing sheep owned by the king. A violent thunderstorm suddenly developed, along with an earthquake that shook the earth and opened up a huge crevasse in the ground. Gyges walked down into the chasm and found, among other amazing things, a hollow bronze horse serving as a coffin for the body of a giant man. The corpse wore a golden ring, which Gyges slipped onto his finger and returned to his daily life.

Soon after, at a dull meeting for shepherds, Gyges began to fiddle with the ring on his finger. He suddenly realized that the other shepherds were talking about him as though he wasn't there. He had turned the top of the ring inward, toward himself and away from the world, rendering him invisible. He turned it back outward and reappeared. He had the power of invisibility in his hands, vanishing with a flip of his ring. His reaction was quick. He talked the other shepherds into letting him bring their annual report to the king. In the palace, he used the power of his ring to seduce the queen, kill the king, and take over the kingdom. Plato tells this story through one of his characters to pose a fundamental question about the roots of moral integrity. Is it possible to be moral in isolation? Can we trust ourselves when we are "invisible," magically or otherwise?

The myth of Gyges, along with the moral deliberations about the story included in Plato's *Republic*, deals with the nature of responsibility. Are we only responsible because we will become unpopular if we are irresponsible? Our morality arises from a wide variety of sources, but is it our own visibility that compels us to be good?

In the familiar story of Genesis, Adam and Eve feel the need to cover and hide their bodies after caving into temptation and eating the forbidden fruit. They hide in the garden to avoid being *seen* by God. Selfishness is safer in the dark, away from probing eyes. God, in Genesis, serves as a "seeing" other for the characters of the first biblical stories. To be seen is to be known and to be riveted to one's actions. Adam looked in vain for invisibility. He settled, apparently, for fig leaves and bushes. The human desire to act without facing responsibility appears to be both ancient and deep.

There are obvious manifestations of this desire in everyday life. How many diet plans simultaneously promise both indulgence and weight loss? How many people fall for the temptation to "buy now and pay later," somehow hoping to delay payment indefinitely? How many hit-and-run accidents litter our highways? How many broken windows are there with no culprit? The temptation to evade responsibility appears among all ages, in all cultures and in remarkably diverse manifestations. The urge to dodge responsibility appears in children at a surprisingly early age. Kids instinctively find ways to dodge responsibility. Children are remarkably adept at passing the buck and shifting blame. One of the greatest challenges of parenting is to guide children to the place where their moral character is based on more than the fear of being caught red-handed. The watchful gazes of relatives and educators are pivotal to moral development, but they can be evaded. Responsibility requires more.

Rules and laws provide guidelines for moral behavior and fair play. But no law is any match for the craftiness of this instinct to avoid responsibility. We deftly avoid responsibility without violating the letter of the law. We can even shield ourselves with the comfort and self-assurance that comes through following a moral code. No set of moral paradigms or rules of behavior can compete with the creative ways we find to fulfill our desires and remain within the law. As a child I was instructed, like most children, not to call my siblings certain names. I instinctively invented my own words, which were mere gibberish, but exactly as effective as the banned vocabulary. When it comes to irritating sisters, "Bornk" seems to work just as well as "idiot."

Plato's clever parable about Gyges addresses a problem that humankind cannot seem to shake. Whatever we say about responsibility, it is undeniable that we humans instinctively seek ways to avoid it. This urge to avoid responsibility, to "twist the ring," poses a formidable obstacle for the pursuit of justice. Though the appearance of these evasions is remarkably diverse, the impulse to sidestep obligations appears to be universal.

Plato tells us that Socrates chimes in shortly after the telling of the story of Gyges. The old philosopher points out that the craftiest people can just *pretend* to be morally upright for the sake of public approval. If clever enough, they can hold high office, wield great power, and still enjoy all the benefits of the cruel and immoral person. Such a person has the cake and eats it too. The words of Socrates would fit quite nicely in an analysis of many politicians, business CEOs, athletes, and even religious leaders of today. A steady diet of scandalous headlines reveals just how many of our celebrities confirm the suspicions voiced by Socrates. They entice us with the appearance of morality and integrity, but behind the scenes they run fast and loose with our lives, our trust, and our money. Even more disturbing is the obvious fact that the best of such swindlers are never caught, going to their graves with the secrets of their deceptions, facade intact.

We can easily take potshots at fallen politicians, pastors, and Enron executives. What is at stake here is more than a critique of high-profile moral failures. The issue at hand is a pressure on responsibility, a force pushing against the human desire to be good. Like Adam and Eve scrambling for cover in the garden, we look for bushes to hide behind. The exposure of being seen captivates and holds us, locking us to our bodies and binding us to our actions and their consequences. This is certainly a positive phenomenon, inasmuch as it holds us fast to responsibilities that we ought not shirk. Still, the fact that we have no magic ring handy does not mean we are completely stripped of the power to disappear.

The problem of *evasion* arises much closer to reality than the fields of film and fiction. We live in a world with countless places to hide from consequences and responsibility. The poignancy of the myth lays not in the fairytale but in the countless opportunities we have for daily evasions of neighbors and their suffering. We are all inclined to hide, to withdraw from the glaring and captivating gaze of others. This evasion of responsibility is one name for evil. The impulse to escape the pressure of responsibility is the urge to become less human and to threaten the humanity of others.

In *The Lord of the Rings*, J. R. R. Tolkien renders the dehumanizing effect of the "ring" quite literally in the transformation of the character Gollum. A deformed and twisted creature who plays an important role in Tolkien's legendary tales, Gollum was once a normal person (perhaps of distant kin to the Hobbits) who knew about love, loyalty, faithfulness, and morality. The power of the ring prolonged his life unnaturally, and he became blind to anything but his desire to have the ring. Tolkien cleverly depicts this character as a split personality. Gollum refers to himself in the plural, as "we" and "us." The pitiful creature can be overheard arguing with himself. The power of hiding had consumed Gollum, but not without something remaining. The man who once knew of friendship and community was forced to seek it internally. His alter ego became his community. The ring had literally dehumanized him, disfiguring him inside and out.

Literal invisibility is the stuff of imagination, of comic books and movies and novels.[2] But these playful fictions are extrapolations of less fantastic evasions common in everyday life. The contortions of Gollum symbolize the dehumanizing effect of internalized existence. Sucked into the seductive power of the ring of invisibility, Gollum is extricated from community. The freedom is intoxicating, but this liberty is bought with a high price. Evading other people removes Gollum from community, which eats away at his very constitution as a person. To act without consequence is surely a charming fantasy, and one that people subtly pursue more often than we care to admit. But success in this venture is perilous. The cost is our very humanity.

Such evasions wreak havoc on the people from whom we hide. Victims of violence, greed, oppression, and discrimination search in vain for a person to hold responsible for their plight. Since we are concerned here with responsibility and its relationship to social justice, it is important to address the temptation of invisibility. Among the most obvious obstacles to justice is evasion. We humans are far too good at it, and apparently we always have been.

Jewish and Christian scriptures abound with examples of ethical evasion. Jacob, a pivotal character in the book of Genesis, is deft in his use of the "ring." His very name translates to "trickster," and Jacob seldom failed to live up to his name.[3] His brother, Esau, was his first victim. Blind with hunger, Esau stumbled back from an unsuccessful hunt and encountered Jacob with a pot of nourishing stew. Jacob smoothly sold the stew to his famished brother in exchange for Esau's rights as a firstborn (see Gen. 25–27). Jacob's craftiest deception may have been the scam he and his mother pulled on his father Isaac. Blinded by old age and reliant on his hearing and touch, Isaac struggled to tell his twin boys apart. So when Jacob approached Isaac to steal his brother's blessing, he wore Esau's clothes and covered his smooth skin with goat hair so Jacob would feel more like his hairy sibling. The deception worked. Jacob turned the ring and fooled his father. He then turned it again, running far away from Esau's angry sword. Evasion was Jacob's first name.

King David "turned the ring" of his wealth to commit murder and adultery, only to have his invisibility unmasked by the prophet Nathan. His evasion of responsibility wrought havoc on his life and legacy but particularly on the lives of others. Money and privilege work well as our modern-day ring of Gyges, just as they effectively supported David's murderous lust. Cash shields us well from the suffering of the world. Credit shields us from responsibility for our own purchases. Many North Americans give no second thought to the sources that provide the products we buy each day. Money provides insulation; we need not be aware that clothing we wear may have been sewn by young children in an overseas sweatshop. We drink our coffee in peace, never forced to see whether our coffee beans were grown by farmers unable to meet basic medical and dental needs. We live away from, and drive around, the parts of the world where suffering and poverty go hand in hand. The things we eat, play with, wear, and enjoy are isolated from their histories. We like it that way.

We also expend significant energy "hiding" from ourselves. It is uncomfortable to survey the damages wrought by actions we have done, or the victims of systems we support. Sometimes the suffering that produces our favorite toys shows through the shiny veneer. In recent years Americans have become aware of the complexity of diamond production, and great lengths have been taken by diamond sellers to verify their product has not been harvested by slaves or exchanged for weaponry. The issue of "conflict diamonds" or "blood diamonds" was hot enough to warrant a Leonardo DiCaprio movie. Other causes are less sexy.

Many major companies have come under fire from activists who point out that low costs in the United States are made possible by deplorable international working conditions. The nature of market competition makes workers vulnerable to exploitation around the world. In response, countries pass legislation that protects workers by preventing child labor, ensuring safe working conditions, and prescribing a reasonable minimum wage. But in places like Vietnam, China, Cambodia, India, Mexico, and Brazil these laws are absent or ignored. Some North American companies remain intentionally ignorant of the reasons for the low cost of imports.

The problem becomes even murkier when we try to rectify our inadequate knowledge of the human suffering that makes products in North America inexpensive. Clothing factories rarely wish to disclose their labor practices. Student groups at several universities around the United States have attempted to trace the clothing sold in their college stores. The task is difficult; in many cases the chain of supply is intentionally obscured. Sales of apparel with university logos account for $2.5 billion of business each year.[4] Though this is a small portion of the total revenue for apparel, it represents a form of labor that is easily outsourced and shifted from one factory to another in search of the lowest cost. The distinguishing aspect of this apparel is the university logo, not the quality or source of the article. A hat bearing a university logo might sell in the school store for $20, of which the university receives $1.50 and the laborer who made the cap about $.08. Eight American cents means something quite different in Cambodia than it does in California, but the possibility of exploitation is clear.

By the year 2000 many student groups discovered their schools were directly tied to sweatshop labor. Students organized rallies and protests at Duke University, Penn State, the University of Oregon, the University of Kentucky, and several others.[5] Some students participated in hunger strikes and sit-ins to draw attention to the glaring inconsistency between university policy and practice. By 2008, 175 colleges and universities in the United States and Canada had joined the Worker Rights Consortium, a group committed to full disclosure of the chain of clothing supply.

Global economics are complex, and the issues involving payment and working conditions should not be oversimplified. Even the most exploitive labor practices bring some economic benefit to employees. But for the most part, when we pick goods off the shelf at the market, we quietly hope that someone else has already taken responsibility for these concerns. Disney, Nike, and Gap have all come under fire for using international factories with deplorable conditions. Fortunately, all three companies have responded to protests by establishing divisions dedicated to safeguarding factory conditions. By 2006 Gap had a workforce of ninety-two employees dedicated to checking and rechecking its factory conditions.[6] One could cynically claim that this "progress" is chiefly related to concerns for maintaining a "good name" for their brand. Their ring of Gyges has been forcibly turned outward in some cases, exposing the suffering behind their products. Who would buy Disney clothing if consumers imagine the broken fingers of children when they look at Mickey's famous ears? But these improvements are encouraging, whatever the motivation. Sadly, many companies, including mega-retailer Walmart, have been reluctant to take these expensive steps to safeguard the well-being of international employees.

Responsibility, as we have noted, is expensive; few people or organizations are quick to voluntarily part with their money. The Mattel toy company lobbied against tighter scrutiny on the lead content of the paint used on their toys, shortly before being forced to make massive recalls of their products to address health risks to consumers.[7] Predatory lenders have found it surprisingly easy to take advantage of immigrants, legal or otherwise. Other examples are more obvious and absurd, such as tobacco companies fighting warning labels and defending their rights to advertise to minors. In the tug-of-war between human suffering and financial profit, cash routinely gets the upper hand.

Perhaps we can be sympathetic for bewildered consumers; how can lone individuals act as a moral compass for the multibillion dollar companies? We justifiably desire that these institutions take responsibility for their own behavior. But a basic, embarrassing fact about humankind is that people and institutions routinely *hide* from their responsibilities. In a global market, the more times commodities change hands, the more difficult it is to trace fault for inhumane working conditions. In this case, the impersonal nature of money acts as the ring of Gyges. Such hiding often includes forms of self-deception. Not all oppression is intentional. We will address the question of intentionality, a concept often tied to responsibility, in an upcoming chapter.

For now it is important to underscore one of the primary ways we sidestep responsibility. The sufferings of the world are often invisible to us. We are busy, or too far behind on paying off private debts, to devote time and energy to human suffering worldwide. We make feeble gestures at charity, giving small slivers of our income to address gaping problems in the world.

Given the temptation to evade and the ease with which we shift and shirk responsibility, what measures can we take to avoid our addiction to the ring of Gyges? This question leads us back to the heart of ethics and the roots of our struggle for justice. If only doing away with the "ring" of evasion was as simple as Tolkien's volcanic fire, which finally consumed Gollum and his precious ring. Tolkien barely conceals his ultimate referendum on invisibility: even the noblest of characters falter. But our own confrontations with the ring-of-evasion, which creates and supports injustice, is much more complicated than the travails of the fictional Middle Earth. We must do more than name and discuss the phenomenon of ethical evasion. The question at hand regards the height of responsibility. Just how responsible am I for the suffering of another? This, too, is an ancient question.

It is one of the oldest questions, in fact, judging by the story we find in Gen. 4. God is interrogating Cain, who recently killed his brother Abel. Like a good *Law and Order* suspect, Cain dodges the question and asks one of his own. These words echo across the pages of human history: "Am I my brother's keeper?" (v. 9). The attempt at sarcasm is palpable; Cain mocks the insinuation that he should be responsible for his brother's location. Should he really be considered responsible for the everyday events of Abel's life? Cain has flipped the ring inward, attempting to hide the blood on his hands. He struggles to disconnect his actions from their consequence. The irony of his question is that in trying to hide from his own history he presupposes that he is *not* responsible for Abel's daily well-being. Cain's question is laced with the assumption that it is absurd to consider him responsible for something as petty as his brother's whereabouts. Cain's unanswered question leaves us wondering: To what level of responsibility are we held?

There is an audacious possibility that the answer to Cain's question is *yes* and that aside from not murdering his brother he was also responsible to be Abel's *keeper*. To such a level of responsibility one could never be worthy. A good person, if very dedicated, might manage to avoid hurting his or her neighbors. But Cain's unanswered question leaves us to wonder whether he is to protect Abel against snakes and bandits and potholes *wherever he may be*. Such responsibility would surely exceed the realm of possibility. Nobody could be that responsible. The impossibility of responsibility may represent the most important and intriguing of all mysteries.

For like Gyges, we face the world with the familiar power of disappearance temptingly close to our fingertips.

three

TERRITORIAL RIGHTS

CHALKY DIRT stuck to the roof of my mouth as I stood on an empty soccer field, face-to-face with the boy who had just taken away my soccer ball. The Saturday afternoon trip to the park to play soccer had taken a turn for the worse. I was eleven years old, perhaps sixty pounds, and standing opposite a classic childhood bully. I had done nothing to provoke the attack. At first, he threatened to keep the ball, which seemed to me like a good deal if it meant I left with all my teeth. But then, when he realized I might depart unscathed, he decided that maybe he'd keep my bicycle. That was the last straw, the prized possession of my preadolescent life. Them was fightin' words!

I looked for a way to get around him, to secure my bike, and be on my way. Wise to me, he bent down to the ground and drew a long line in the sand with his muscular finger. "This bike is mine now; you step over this line and I'll kill you." I didn't actually believe he'd kill me, but I was rather worried about my teeth, having just finished growing them. The line taunted me as much as he did. The proverbial "line in the sand" was literal, in this case. The smell of the dust hung in my nose. And I stepped.

The "territory" he established in drawing the line was entirely arbitrary. The sand on one side of that line is very much the same city playground property as the sand on the other. The young man, who eventually exchanged my bicycle for the privilege of blackening my eye, named part of the territory his own. He then put up his dukes and waited for battle. It is in the realm of possessions and territory that we find remarkable insight into the concept of responsibility. Literally and figuratively, we draw lines around our lives, possessions, and interests and bare our teeth at those who come near our borders. Some of these boundaries are healthy and appropriate and vital. But other boundaries are exclusive, biased, confrontational, defensive, and selfish. Once the lines have been drawn we feel justified in defending our territory; if you move into someone else's space, you can expect to pay for it. The playground and the battleground are not nearly as far apart as they may seem.

My childhood foe was particularly unreasonable in his line drawing, though perhaps no less reasonable than the European settlers who colonized North America. The colonists, often justifying their behavior by dehumanizing native peoples, systematically stripped the first inhabitants of land and property. Treaties were violated and rewritten, battles were waged, and blood was spilt. The most brazen and irresponsible kind of line drawing dares to differentiate between who can be considered *human* and who cannot. A sad legacy of human history is the seemingly endless cycle of dehumanizing and genocidal behavior. For some early settlers of North America, including the Puritans, it was all too easy to repeat the dehumanizing behavior they had tried to leave behind in Europe. Despite the Thanksgiving mythology celebrated every November, the Puritans typically depicted the Native Americans as half-human and half-devil.[1]

The native people were utterly foreign to the settling Europeans, and the vast differences in language and culture bred fear. Once the colonists had successfully established that the native nations were on the other side of the line that separates humans from nonhumans, it was all too easy to treat them like animals. The result was, and remains, appalling. The centuries that followed the first Thanksgiving were filled with atrocious examples of dehumanization and bloodthirsty massacre.

In 1864, as the abolition of slavery was being finalized in the United States, the genocidal attitude toward native people raged on. Colonel John Chivington led the infamous Sand Creek Massacre in Colorado that spring. Racial tensions reached a feverish level during the battles that led up to the incidents at Sand Creek. Facing defeat, the Cheyenne leader Black Kettle raised a white flag in submission. Chivington refused to honor the surrender and ordered a charge. The carnage that followed is infamous and legendary, most of it too graphic to reprint here. They slaughtered scores of elderly people, children, pregnant women, and unarmed members of the

Cheyenne and Arapaho nations. They went further, disfiguring and maiming the dead; Chivington appeared on stage in Denver carrying body parts hacked from his victims.[2]

Chivington was a lay preacher, a prominent Methodist in good standing. Those who study history often marvel at the ability of religious people to own slaves, support genocide, and massacre the defenseless. A clue to the mentality of the colonel is found in the slogan attributed to Chivington by one of his soldiers and often quoted afterward: "Kill 'em all, big and small," he cried. *"Nits make lice."*[3] The native people had become as insignificant as insects to this colonel, and they were treated as such by him and his soldiers. Chivington and his troops managed to draw a line that excluded his enemy from the realm of humanity. With effective, charismatic line drawing, a leader can motivate followers to do almost anything.

The people of precolonial North America should not be romanticized; they were not always gentle, and their nations were not always peaceful. We are most interested here in the philosophy that made possible this attempted genocide. The ethical tool used by the European settlers was *line drawing*. They were responsible to treat other human beings with civility. They drew clever lines defining who counted as human and who did not. The native nations of North America found themselves on the wrong side of that line.

Most attempts at genocide, modern and ancient, follow a similar pattern. The logic used to dehumanize the ethnic groups native to North America bears striking resemblance to the tools used to support the institution of slavery in the United States. The lines drawn to separate people by ethnicity are stark in the pages of early American law books; a different set of rules for a different shade of melanin. The embarrassing pro-slavery legislation is clear: people of African descent can be owned, but people of European descent cannot. In 1787, the House of Representatives decided to consider slaves "three-fifths" of a person for the sake of census and taxation.[4] The bloodshed of the Civil War was the product of a cataclysmic clash between philosophies of line drawing. The Southern states scratched a line in the sand, sometimes called the Mason-Dixon Line, and dared the Northern states to encroach.

Boundary marking is directly related to responsibility. We constantly draw and redraw boundaries to adjust, restrict, and extend the scope of our responsibilities. Across history, women have often been victims of this sinister form of line drawing. With frightening ease, countless civilizations and cultures have drawn a line between genders and considered one gender superior to the other. This usually means that one gender is credited as more capable of doing things that matter for society. In rare instances we have observed matriarchal societies, where women hold higher authority than men. But in the vast majority of cultures, women have been considered inferior. Often they have been considered less than fully human. This line drawing has justified the ownership of women as property, the mistreatment and abuse of female bodies, and the constant preference for males in positions of leadership. It should strike today's generation as truly remarkable that as recently as 1919 women were turned away from ballot boxes in the United States because their gender disqualified them from casting a vote. To become superior to a neighbor, enemy, or even one's own mother, one need only be very good at drawing lines.

We might be tempted to turn for help to the towering giants of Western ethics, the geniuses who crafted ethical theory and set out careful guidelines for humane interactions. David Hume, John Locke, Immanuel Kant, and other European thinkers outlined the bedrock moral structures for contemporary society, including the basics of modern democracy. But in the writings of each of these thinkers we find clear signs of racism and sexism. Hume claimed, "Negroes were naturally inferior to whites."[5] Kant considered natives of America and Africa "lower in their mental capacities than other races."[6] John Locke deeply influenced the Declaration of Independence and famously argued that human beings are "blank slates" for the impressions of culture and education. Nevertheless, he classified Native Americans as mentally inferior, to be classed with "children and idiots."[7] Perhaps this dulls the luster of the so-called geniuses of Western ethics, but it certainly does not negate all of the valuable contributions they have made to morality. Surely it also means that nobody is immune to the kind of sinister line drawing that leads to slavery, genocide, sexism, and oppression.

Hitler's atrocities began with a steady, rhythmic progression of anti-Semitic laws. In the first six years he was in power, four hundred laws were passed that eventually restricted every aspect of the lives of German Jews.[8] Hitler's rise was driven by line drawing, as he systematically created literal and ideological lines to rewire a national understanding of responsibility.

So here we find ourselves adept at another skill, and one that is not particularly conducive to justice. There seems to be a basic human desire to be on the happy side of the line, where the grass is green and the living easy. We seem to instinctively consider what is *native* to our lives and environment superior to that which is alien, or *other*. The consequences of this desire to be superior are dire; we feel empowered to draw lines around our territory and then protect it from all attackers. We also routinely fail to analyze the lines we inherit from generations before us and from scars and experiences in our pasts.

The power of these inherited lines is obvious in the borderlands of our world. Gone are the days when ethnic groups maintained distinct boundaries. Our cities are a tapestry of cultures and ethnicities, all collected into tight and tense urban spaces. We inherit hoards of stereotypes, reinforced by fear, and small incidents quickly escalate toward violence. Racial tension remains one of the most stubborn problems in the world today, as our shrinking planet confronts extreme diversity. No longer can we hide behind the lines our ancestors drew to keep the stranger and the alien at a distance. Our lives now crash inevitably into one another. The old lines of ancestral prejudice are now reduced to a complicated maze of stereotypes that serve to reinforce both violence and fear.

Those whose space has been violated feel deeply justified in violent, often incommensurate, retaliation. People are comfortable on their home turf, in their own property, or on familiar grounds. Our sense of territory runs deep and must certainly relate to a very good need and desire to protect our relatives and loved ones. But we must beware: how very easy it is to draw lines in such a way that they benefit us, and then punish anyone who does not agree.

The territorial tendencies in human nature are fundamental to our sense of responsibility. We feel the need to be responsible for home, homeland, friends, and family. The desire to protect "me and mine" is steadily infected by the competitive drive for more, an impulse we will examine in detail in the next chapter. The right to "the pursuit of happiness" is joined with the right to draw lines wider and wider around one's estate and influence. This can snowball, redoubling injustice and exploiting every loophole in the name of expansion and increase. There are no rules, of course, to regulate how rich or famous one may become, nor how wide one's territory can extend. Along with each new set of financial and territorial gains comes the right to defend them against anyone who might want a slice.

It must be underscored that boundary making and line drawing should not be considered intrinsically evil. Bodies should not be violated, homes should not be robbed, and privacy should not be invaded. This chapter is deeply and directly concerned with the violation of good and appropriate lines that serve to protect the weak and those who suffer. We are concerned here with victimization, with understanding the forces within human nature and culture that seem to drive us to overstep our boundaries. Certainly measures should be taken to safeguard vulnerable people. And these measures represent one form of healthy line drawing. To establish that no person should be enslaved or that women should never be considered inferior to men is to *redraw* offensive lines, not to obliterate them.

Before turning to some intriguing passages of Scripture for wisdom on the question of boundaries and territory, we must point out that even some of the great theologians of Christian history have made dreadful mistakes in their line drawing. Across the centuries of Western and Christian thinking about morality, countless "maps" have been drawn, each ranking and prioritizing various aspects of human life. Poorly drawn maps are not always an indication of malicious or selfish behavior. We might even be generous enough to say that great thinkers like Augustine, Thomas Aquinas, and Martin Luther constructed the best maps they could, given their positions in time, culture, and history. But this does not change the troubling problems that appear in their atlases of theology, philosophy, and ethics. Their wholehearted commitment to Christianity does not ensure they are faultless guides in our pursuit of responsibility.

Luther provides us with a vivid and troubling example. He shook the landscape of the Western world in his bold and audacious attempts to reform Christianity. His insistence on the importance of faith, grace, and Scripture changed more than just Christianity. Luther shook political landscapes, giving rise to new ways of thinking about authority, oppression, race, and gender. Early in his career, Luther seemed to think that Jews were put off by the oppressive and legalistic tone of Roman Christianity. He was confident that once Jews saw his purified version of the Christian gospel they would eagerly convert. As his career progressed, Luther became less and less patient with Jews and their unwillingness to embrace even the Protestant version of Jesus' message. One of the great embarrassments of Luther's life and career is the vitriolic anti-Semitism that seems to have resulted from these frustrations. In one of the most frightening theological treatises ever written, Luther calls Jews a "base, whoring people."[9] He claimed that Jews were venomous snakes, good for nothing more than forced labor. Their money and property were to be taken from them.[10] Jewish synagogues, homes, and schools should be burned to the ground. Not only does Luther advocate the murder of Jews, he even claims that Christians "are at fault for not slaying them."[11]

All of this from the man whose genius has inspired billions of people to reconsider the depth of grace and the wonder of the Christian cross? Luther radically reconfigured the map of Christian theology, but he drew a few lines on his map that had disastrous consequences for the twentieth century. There is some scholarly debate about the nature of the influence of Martin Luther on Adolf Hitler. There is an uncanny and chilling resemblance between Luther's genocidal attitude toward Jews and the rhetoric of the Third Reich. We are wise to be suspicious of the ways that maps have been drawn. Luther is an extreme example; often the mapping mistakes are subtle and less easy to identify. But we are wise to be on guard against this cunning and effective method of altering the structure of responsibility. One can get away with anything, even murder, if one can draw the lines right.

This impulse is not foreign to Christian and Jewish scripture. Line drawing and boundary protection are crucial aspects of both ancient and modern life. In Deuteronomy we find an intriguing repetition, in the midst of the unfolding ethical paradigms that become the backbone of the Hebrew scriptures. The phrase "remember that you were a slave in Egypt" is repeated five times in Deuteronomy (5:15; 15:15; 16:12; 24:18, 22). Interestingly, this reverberating reminder appears in a wide variety of situations. In each of the manifestations the application is clear: Israelites can never forget that they were once *on the other side of the line*. In 5:14-15 the Israelites are reminded to give rest to servants and animals on the Sabbath. Why? Because they were once mistreated slaves in Egypt. Even foreigners, with no commitment to Sabbath observance, are to be given rest. It would be easy for Israel to draw a line, preserving the rest of Sabbath for those who qualify on the basis of race and religion. But they must never forget what it means to be oppressed, lest they become oppressors.

The refrain shows up throughout Deuteronomy, culminating in chapter 24, which uses the phrase twice. Here the legislation turns to address the temptation to "pervert" justice on behalf of those who are voiceless and vulnerable. Law and custom normally allow lenders to take some collateral to insure they will be repaid. But verses 17-18 forbid lenders to hold a widow's clothing in pledge against her debts. The poor and the needy make easy targets for oppression; they have no resources to organize a protest and can do very little about injustice. The hired hand, who is "poor and needy," should be paid promptly and generously (v. 14). Why? Israel must remember: "you were a slave in Egypt" (v. 18). It is easy to adjust legal and moral lines to take advantage of people whose voices lack volume. Israel is never to forget what it feels like to be powerless and voiceless.

The final reiteration of this phrase pertains to the harvesting of fields. When people harvest their crops, a good amount of the produce goes ungathered after the first pass. It takes at least two harvestings to fully glean a field. But verses 21-22 forbid a second pass. The leftovers are to remain on the field for widows, orphans, and foreigners. It is the inclusion of the alien, in particular, which makes this theme most surprising. Much of the rest of the Hebrew Bible is concerned with the dangers associated with the alien, who often came bearing idols or weapons to threaten Israel and its worship. So we should at least pause at this unusual gesture of hospitality. Are Israelites really responsible to feed their enemies? To nourish those who would contaminate their land with the worship of foreign gods?

These commands from Deuteronomy become increasingly shocking when they are aligned with some of the other ethical codes from antiquity. There were several collections of laws to guide behavior in the ancient Near East; these legal codes are sometimes similar to the Torah and sometimes very different. The most famous of these compilations is the Code of Hammurabi, which scholars date to the eighteenth century BCE. Though many laws and commands bear passing resemblance to the words of Deuteronomy, there is no sign of any parallel to the compassion commanded to servants, widows, and foreigners.[12] Many of the commandments we find in the Torah are logical and straightforward. Like the Code of Hammurabi, they encourage behaviors that lead to survival and social health and prohibit activities that cause suffering and disruption. But Deut. 24 is both innovative and dangerous.

There is something unique, impractical, and even dangerous about this commandment to leave food in the fields for the least important cogs in the social wheel. The application for our understanding of responsibility is straightforward. Israel is responsible for the food, shelter, and well-being of its poor, its destitute, and even its enemies. The impulse to draw lines of exclusion is to be resisted. Farmers are to limit their profits in respect for the plight of the widow, the poor, and even the foreigner. The farmer may have every right to build tall walls to keep the field safe from plunder; but these legitimate rights are questioned on behalf of the hungry. The people of Israel must remember that they, too, once hungered.

Responsibility at this level is impractical, exceeding the boundaries of what can be expected of anyone. One might be surprised that even animals are to receive rest and compassion on the Sabbath. But it is truly shocking to find allowance for enemies. Compassion to my neighbor comes with perks; when I need help, she may remember I was there for her. Ethicists Thomas Hobbes, Jean-Jacques Rousseau, and John Locke claimed that this is the source of all ethical customs. People do "good" to one another in exchange for a society where others will reciprocate. But the commands of Deuteronomy dream beyond the contractual structure of economic exchange. One is likely to get burned for acting kindly toward the dangerous alien. The command to feed the stranger beckons beyond the commerce and struggle of the world. It harkens to a call for responsibility beyond typical reason and logic. But perhaps only responsibility this scandalous can address a world this broken.

This theme was not lost on Jesus, who spun the remarkable tale of the Good Samaritan in response to the question: "Who is my neighbor?" (Luke 10:25-37). In Jesus' parable, a beaten Israelite lies dying in the ditch. Two men pass their bloody countryman, despite their obvious ethnic ties to the victim. For whatever reason, they are able to justify an evasion of responsibility, scurrying down the road and leaving the man to die. The Samaritan has legitimate ethnic reasons to avoid the suffering Israelite. Relations between Israel and Samaria were often tense; many members of these two ethnic groups would rejoice to see the other suffer. But this man, who would not be technically considered responsible for the man in the ditch, is the very "neighbor" who takes responsibility. At considerable risk and expense, the Samaritan accepted responsibility for suffering he neither caused nor found himself legally obligated to address.

The ironic twist in Jesus' story echoes the illogical hospitality of Deuteronomy. Responsibility exceeds the logic of commerce and fairness. It exceeds the matrix of rights and territory we naturally associate with our obligations. Responsibility defies evasion.

Cain underestimated; he was to be keeper for more than just his brother.

four

HOUSE RULES

A LITERAL ninety-eight-pound weakling, I found my fifteen-year-old body unable to compete with my much larger peers in most sports. The solution, I discovered, was wrestling. In wrestling, as in boxing, judo, tae kwon do, and other sports, athletes only compete against opponents of similar weight. For me, this evened the playing field and allowed me some measure of success. There is something primitive about the sport of wrestling, along with other forms of hand-to-hand combat. No equipment or technology can give one athlete an advantage over another. It is a raw battle to overcome, to pin an opponent humiliatingly to the ground. To be victorious, a person must combine wit and strength. Perhaps the oldest sport in the world, each match resembles countless battles before it. Unsurprisingly, competitive wrestling arose in a wide range of cultures around the world. Early civilizations in Mesopotamia, Japan, Egypt, Greece, and Rome all idolized the champion's struggle for supremacy. The fundamentals of battle, war, and competition are at the heart of the wrestler's struggle.

War, for all of its horror and goriness, is less foreign to daily life than it seems. We may be fortunate to live far away from battle lines and flying explosives, but the logic of war is never far away. Human bodies are wired to fight for survival, built to struggle for the continued existence of our communities. The wrestler's struggle mirrors the fundamental human desire to survive and dominate. It is a short leap to apply our time-honed skills of conflict to the daily struggle for money, time, love, and happiness. In fact, we import many of these survival skills into our everyday interactions. Evidence abounds, perhaps most vividly on the toy shelves of our children. Game after game promotes and encourages aggression and even violence as the quickest and most effective resolution to problems and disputes. Otherwise violent events, such as "sinking battleships" or "eliminating enemies," are the most exciting and pivotal features of these games. Hasbro, whose motto is "Making the world smile," markets a toy called the Gun Sniper to kindergartners.[1] When babies peer over the edge of their cribs at the world that awaits them, the tools and reasoning of war are ready and waiting.

There is a debate raging between parent groups and the manufacturers of toys and video games regarding the way these activities influence children. But whether or not playing these games translates directly into violent behavior, we can certainly see that the methods of conflict resolution that underwrite war are familiar to even our youngest children. Aggression works well in winning competitive children's games, not to mention the games adults play. Strength, violence, and aggression are self-validating. As in war, the bigger guns and most deceitful schemers are most likely to win, and the thrill of victory validates the methods of conquest. This is the rule-book for survival, and it is useful when trying out for sports, landing that coveted job, getting high grades, and even winning the heart of that special someone. We are designed to struggle and fight for victory; each of us descended from a long line of ancestors who won the battle for survival. We are born and bred to win. This means we are also acutely aware of the many ways to exploit the weaknesses of others. As in war, the way to win almost every contest is to take advantage of a hole in the defenses of the opposition. And here we find our instincts to survive at odds with responsibility.

Certainly these heroes of war and athleticism embody an extreme expression of something about the human spirit that can be counted as good. We build our homes, lives, and communities on determination and resolve. Our lives and accomplishments are driven by this desire to win, to surpass, to succeed, to gain in power and prestige. When this fire fades inside of us, we may slide toward laziness and underachievement. The desire that drives the wrestler, the parent, the inventor, and the astronaut must be seen as a rich and necessary core to human existence. For the engine of humanity, desire is the fuel. But how much should we admire the strength, power, and dominance of those who win the battles and stand atop the podium?

There are a host of obvious problems that arise from the powerful desire that drives human actions. In many of its manifestations this desire takes the form of hostility, the very opposite of hospitality. The other person appears before the self as competition, as threat, as an object for conquest or possession. Those who succeed in sport and in war are praised for their ability to hone their skills with the rigors of hostility. The same could easily be said for the most successful traders on Wall

Street. These champions are decorated for something quite different from the ideals of hospitality and responsibility. We must ask ourselves, for the sake of the majority who lose the fight for power: "What does *desire* have to do with justice?"

One option might be to consider success, force, and victory the key measure of what is good. This is similar to the controversial suggestions of Friedrich Nietzsche, a nineteenth-century philosopher who challenged most of the traditional assumptions about goodness and morality. Nietzsche celebrated the desire for power, which seems to stir the hearts of strong people. For Nietzsche, this "will to power" is a part of humanity's rich past and glorious future. Nietzsche placed a high value on the displays of force that win wars and vanquish enemies. He mocked bullies, who cower before the powerful but pick on the weak. He admired the spirit of the champion, who accepts no less than victory and offers no excuses in defeat.

The world has not remembered Friedrich Nietzsche fondly, and to be honest, he probably earned most of this legacy. His writings rail against women, pronounce a form of atheism, undermine classical moral codes, and challenge almost every established form of government or religion. Still, philosophers read him widely and consider his philosophical genius to be nearly unparalleled in the history of philosophy. His writings are gritty, controversial, and surprising. Nietzsche's thought has inspired a diverse following, and virtually everyone who engages the field of philosophy crosses paths with Nietzsche's work. Nevertheless, nobody fully embraces his project and eccentric opinions.

Despite all of this, Nietzsche arrives at the question of responsibility with such a unique perspective that he becomes an invaluable companion for those who ask questions about morality. Nietzsche is no friend to the brand of other-centered responsibility this book is proposing. But sometimes one's friends are all too willing to overlook one's shortcomings. Nietzsche has no such reservations.

Nietzsche's first love is the classical Greek tragedy. In Greek tragedy heroes struggle mightily against fate and against enemies to achieve great glory. The great Greek poets and mythmakers prized the valiant struggle for power and dominion. In Homer's world brave sailors and warriors battle for property, wealth, women, and wisdom. Their actions are often full of arrogance and self-assertion. Sometimes a hero will take on an enemy, monster, or even a god just to prove his valor. To be great is to be a conqueror and to rise above the clingy cries for sympathy and peace that plague the masses. Heracles, perhaps the ultimate model of Greek masculinity and heroism, took on a host of monsters and enemies in a remarkable display of wit and valor. His twelve labors, performed as penance for killing his family, are a massive display of supremacy; lions, boars, birds, and monsters all collapse at the feet of the clever and mighty Heracles.

In these epic stories, to suffer is to show weakness and to be great is to become increasingly impervious to suffering. Nietzsche believed that Platonic philosophy, as well as its stepchild Christianity, had lost this love for the tragic and bold hero. He thought that by teaching people to embrace their stations in life rather than challenge their superiors, Christianity was numbing and muting the most beautiful aspect of human life.[2] Nietzsche loved the smoldering fire that stirs in the heart of every human to challenge superiors, to beat the odds, to risk everything, and even to defy heaven itself. This fire, perhaps best labeled *desire*, encourages humans to reach for their highest aspirations and dream their boldest dreams. Some people, by Nietzsche's estimation, are better than others at striving for their dreams. The world belongs to people such as these.

Compassion and other-centeredness function, for Nietzsche, as weaknesses that might keep the ultimate heroes from achieving the unfettered future they desired. Such "masters" of the universe write their own moral code, rather than letting the weak and powerless determine how they ought to be treated. Greek mythology is thick with this kind of dominating behavior. Many Greek myths include a son killing his father; patricide is the ultimate rejection of authority. Brazen Prometheus defies the gods by stealing fire, risking everything and then willingly accepting his torturous punishment. The only wrong way to live, for Nietzsche and these ancient Greek heroes, is to live cowardly and uneventfully. To truly live is to seize the brass ring of destiny, at whatever cost. In Homer's epic poem *The Illiad* the great hero Achilles is given the choice to either live a short life of fame and valor or a long life of quiet happiness. Initially Achilles leans toward the long and happy life, but the death of his friend and the allure of war guide Achilles to making the choice for glory and fame. His death, by poison arrow to his vulnerable heel, is the price he pays for his everlasting fame.

Nietzsche found in these ancient heroes a sense of destiny and aggression he thought was woefully absent from modern existence. The Western world, as Nietzsche saw it, had grown soft and sedated under the spell of Platonism and Christianity.[3] At heart, Nietzsche loved humanity for what it might become and for the unlimited potential of the human race. But he saw in Christianity the very shackles that hold humanity back from its glorious future. Christianity encourages compassion and pity, the very softness than prevents us from fulfilling our glorious potential.

Cruel as he sounds, Nietzsche has aptly described the environment common to wrestling mats, school playgrounds, marketplaces, and football fields. There is no limitation to how many yards one can gain in a given football game or how many dollars can be made on the stock exchange. Only a fool would feel compassionate for the linebacker or stop to help a defender who has stumbled and fallen. Few stock traders would stop trading simply to leave more money on the table for someone else to snatch up. For his part, Nietzsche at least rejects the impulse to hoard resources; Nietzsche opposes greed as ferociously as he opposes Christianity. But the ultimate weakness, the one that holds back humanity the most, is *pity*. Nietzsche has no patience for compassionate concern for the defeated, the weak, and the lowly.

In a remarkable number of our everyday interactions, we play by Nietzsche's rules, the rules of the gladiator and Greek champion. There are some subtle conventions about fair play and honesty that sometimes dictate our interactions. But seldom is compassion a virtue in competition. Many professional athletes testify that they are drawn to their sports by the appeal of hand-to-hand combat with a discernable winner and loser. Aggression is encouraged. To a degree, it is also considered admirable to humiliate one's opponent, which somehow underscores the superior skills of the victor. But the realm of athletics does not cherish cruelty. One is only "cruel" to achieve a higher objective than compassion or love: victory.

In this world, as in Nietzsche's, indifference to the suffering of others is not virtuous but simply a necessary aspect of being victorious. Perhaps it is even more glorious to achieve victory without cruelty, like a crafty football running back that manages to score untouched. One seldom wins a race by caring about the feelings of those who cannot win. For Nietzsche, this is the *tragic* sense of life. Not everybody gets to win, and we all have to deal with our own destiny to be both winners and losers in the fight for power. For Nietzsche, to be noble is to embrace life for its tragic highs and lows. J. K. Rowling injected Nietzschean philosophy into one of the characters of her best-selling Harry Potter series. "There is no good and evil," mused the sinister Quirinus Quirrell. "There is only power, and those too weak to seek it."[4]

A more poignant example is certainly the way unfettered capitalism functions in human societies. Laissez-faire (French for "leave it alone") capitalism attempts to place no restriction on the accumulation of wealth by those who are crafty and industrious enough to win the battle of the market. In this sort of economy, financial morality is rarely considered; it is up to the people with money to decide how to spend it and what ought to restrict their own accumulation of wealth. Though outright stealing might be frowned upon, just about any other method by which one might accumulate wealth is acceptable. This is not the form of capitalism that is practiced in the United States. American capitalism is restricted by regulations that attempt to protect consumers, small businesses, and the potential victims of rough-and-tumble capitalistic practices. Familiar manifestations of these restrictions include protections against monopolies, taxation to support social services, and laws forbidding scams and pyramid moneymaking schemes.

To the creative entrepreneur, however, these laws and regulations merely serve as sidelines and rules for the grand game of capitalism. So while Warren Buffett and Bill Gates must play fair, the biggest prize is still the accumulation of wealth. This does not mean, of course, that people who play the game of capitalism are ruthless and heartless; Buffet and Gates are among the more generous and influential citizens in the world. Still, money and power go hand in hand, and big companies know how to lean on legislators to create a setting that maximizes capital. Effective companies are also adept at manipulating customers through advertising and product presentation. Though capitalism leaves abundant room for compassion and justice, it hands out very few awards for such behavior.

Like many children, my own introduction to capitalism was underscored by Parker Brother's best-selling board game Monopoly. Played by more than a half billion people in the last century, Monopoly offers players an opportunity to combine chance and skill in their quest to accumulate all the cash and gain control of all properties.[5] The game winner, for those with enough patience to endure the game to the finish, is the last player standing. Though players must follow certain rules, such as paying medical bills, spending time in jail, and paying rent, the successful competitor overcomes these obstacles by managing to dominate the "market," eliminating other players from the game. There is no room for compassion for the plight of those less successful at the capitalistic game. Selling properties for less than market value is suicidal; allowing a player to stay for free on one's property is a violation of the rules of the game. To win at Monopoly is to succeed at Nietzsche's game, to "will to power" with such effectiveness that nothing stands between a player and the manifestation of desire and dominance.

That corner of each person's heart that makes us good at sports or Monopoly is the element of human nature Nietzsche found to be beautiful and admirable. What Nietzsche loathed was anything that imposed itself on the burning fire that leads humans to struggle for supremacy. Religion became one of his favorite whipping posts, since religious precepts regularly encourage people to set aside these desires and be concerned about the welfare of others. Nietzsche earned his share of scorn, to be sure, but beyond his misogyny and angry tirades there is an overlooked accuracy to his claims about human nature. He is regularly rejected for the cruel world he envisions, but in the end we fairly regularly participate in Nietzsche's dream. In the way we play, in the way we live, and in the way we approach responsibility, we drift perilously toward the Nietzschean contest for power and dominance. It should not surprise us that we reap many of the vices that come with this supposed virtue.

To be responsible in capitalistic society is to avoid being wasteful, to succeed at every opportunity to use skill and chance to turn one dollar into two. One loses games and money if one fails to *capitalize* on opportunities. Responsibility is about self-actualization and the maximization of one's potential. This does not mean that one disregards the needs of others or that responsibility does not include obligation to the neighbor. It is, rather, a question of *primacy*. What responsibility is supreme? What form of responsibility is most encouraged? In capitalism, as in athletics, responsibility begins with self-actualization and the fulfillment of personal potential. The neighbor comes second. The enemy? We may never become concerned for the people who struggle against us for the prize.

Such a worldview is clearly riddled with problems. Nietzsche's dream of a world in which people fight tooth and nail for supremacy has been partly realized in modern economics. My critique of capitalism is modest in scope; I am not attempting to propose an alternate economic system. What seems compelling and important for our discussion of responsibility are the kinds of instincts developed in a society and economy that prizes capital. To be responsible is to be efficient, to understand the demand for results and products. To be responsible is to be *true to yourself* and all the potential that lies within your own life.

There is something hollow to this form of responsibility, even as it allows entrepreneurs like Bill Gates to accumulate enormous wealth and thus provide sensational contributions to global justice. The problem with "be true to yourself" is that the self is very good at perceiving the world in whatever way it wishes. The roads to self-fulfillment are littered with the wounded bodies of people who stand in the way. There is merit to being true to oneself; Nietzsche was not all wrong. But we are sometimes frightfully good at fooling ourselves into believing we are acting and living responsibly, even when we are not. The responsibility that begins with being true to oneself is decidedly internal. By Nietzsche's rules, we become judge and jury of our own actions.

It is often easier to pass the buck than to identify one's responsibility for suffering or injustice in the world. The danger is obvious: individual humans become so captivated by their own vision for the future and for the world that they see past the faces that suffer at the hands of these dreams. This has not been the fate of all capitalist systems or capitalistic people, but it certainly represents a dangerous temptation for humans who are good at Monopoly. The results are predictable; as Fyodor Dostoyevsky put it, "With my pitiful earthly

. . . understanding, all I know is that there is suffering and that there are none guilty."[6]

The ways of war are not the ways of justice. "Civilized warfare," an odd term if there ever was one, comes laden with a code of ethics. In our games these take the form of sidelines, rulebooks, and unwritten codes of conduct. In economics the code of ethics takes the form of minimum wage and antitrust laws, among other things. In the classroom atmosphere there are a host of rules and regulations, written and unwritten, designed to make the competition for points and grades equitable. But at the end of the day, these conventions only take on the appearance of a moral code. We can easily confuse moral integrity with adherence to these rulebooks or ethical codes. But the brand of responsibility that is borne along by these systems is pale and sickly. One is obligated to play fair, to win humbly, and to lose gracefully. The guidelines for fair play in society offer a sham ethics, the appearance of goodness without the substance. This weak and hidden sense of morality is the chief opponent of true justice. The "house rules" of fair play are little more than battle guidelines, rules of engagement. Their morality is based on the codes of violence and war. This mentality can hardly be expected to guide us to justice.

Worse yet, the Monopoly rules for responsibility and obligation are among the chief culprits for the cloud of injustice that hangs over the world today. This latent ethics of Western society allows for a constant shifting of responsibility. By bending and manipulating the rules, crafty veterans of this game-for-power learn how to dodge their obligations. But it goes further than evading responsibility. Successful capitalists, like good athletes, exploit for their own advantage every loophole and vulnerability in the system. They find themselves inflicting wounds and charging their victims for the bandages. Compassion is a sideshow, unworthy of the field of play. The fiery drive of competition, so pivotal for survival and production, has a sharp double edge. It threatens our humanity.

The road toward justice and hospitality leads through the heart of humanity's greatest asset and sharpest vice. Desire gets us out of bed in the morning, but it can also make us calloused and indifferent to the way our drive to succeed damages the lives of others. We may be tempted to loathe human desire, to see it as an enemy and attempt to do away with this constant, dissatisfied yearning. It is interesting that Nietzsche attacked Christianity precisely because he thought Christians were taught to hate their own desires and thus run away from their own humanity. My suggestion here is that desire is not to be rejected; it must be transformed to meet the high demands of responsibility. The bottomless nature of desire has been the source of atrocious deeds in human history. But the unlimited nature of our longings may also be the source of profound hope. We live in a world where injustice seems to be unlimited. Perhaps the stirrings of human desire should be understood as exactly the yearning for justice, as unlikely as a just future may seem. Nietzsche was wrong; Christianity affirms the restless desire of the human heart, but redirects it to the suffering other. The hungry fire that can give rise to crooked exploitation can also burn insatiably for justice. Christian desire is restless until all oppression is gone, impatient until all the world is at peace, and hungry until all mouths are fed.

five

BEING ASYLUM

CAUGHT in a vice of greed and framed for the murder of his wife, Dr. Richard Kimble (played by Harrison Ford) is convicted of murder and sentenced to die. The fictional movie *The Fugitive* (1993) depicts Kimble's escape from captivity and his struggle to find the real killer. U.S. Marshals impede his mission, seeking to return him to custody for his eventual execution. Fugitives, whether innocent or guilty, run and hide in nearly the same manner. Kimble becomes the quarry for a manhunt; his innocence or guilt become irrelevant to his pursuers. Cornered at the edge of a towering dam by Samuel Gerard (Tommy Lee Jones), Kimble tells Gerard through clenched teeth: "I did not kill my wife." Gerard's cold response drives Kimble to jump: "I don't care."

People have been running from justice since prehistory. Expert hunters have pursued these fugitives like prey. Societies employ people like Gerard to catch those who attempt to evade trial and punishment. Gerard and most others who share his profession are not paid to play judge or jury. Their job is to bring the criminal back, in a body bag if necessary. One of the creative twists invoked by the makers of *The Fugitive* is to pit two "good guys" against one another. Tommy Lee Jones won an Oscar for the performance, masterfully winning audiences over with his determined chase. After all, we admire heroes who do hard jobs in difficult times. Somebody has to hunt down fugitives; we like to think that real-world investigators are as tenacious as Gerard. But his character's tenacity is frightening alongside the potential innocence of the man he pursues. Ford invites us to empathize with his character, an "everyman" thrown into a horrific nightmare.

In early human history, the leaders of tribal society lacked the modern tools of imprisonment and transport. Capital punishment was the only method that could reasonably ensure that murderers or rapists would not repeat their crimes. In ancient Israel, the job of hunting down fugitives often fell to the family of the victims. A relative of the deceased would be named the "kinsmen avenger" and sent to find and execute the criminal.[1] The retributive vengeance would be performed with immunity. The kinsmen avenger could torture and execute the fugitive without any consequences. Justice was therefore swift and final when it was enacted. The cloud of injustice that hangs over a family or a society is cleared with the blood of the criminal. An eye is exchanged for an eye. It is clever legislation; the people most disturbed by the crime are the ones who have the opportunity to spill the blood of the criminal. But what if the fugitive is innocent?

Virtually every human community we can find, modern or ancient, has developed a moral prohibition against murder.[2] But even on this question we find a great deal of ambiguity. How provoked must someone be before his or her actions no longer qualify as murder? This differs between cultures and countries, and sometimes must be decided on a case-by-case basis. But there is even greater ambiguity when the question of *intentionality* is raised. What about accidents that cause unintentional death? Our modern world abounds with these instances of manslaughter. With no hint of malicious intentions, doctors prescribe the wrong dosage, cars crash, hunting weapons misfire, and a host of other incidents cause accidental deaths.

How responsible should people be for deaths they cause by misfortune? The plights of both the manslayer and the innocent fugitive drive to the heart of our discussion about responsibility. Accidental deaths create a great wave of pain and suffering that have no obvious or sinister source. On the question of manslaughter we are fortunate to find a surprising and extended treatment of the concept in Scripture, with remarkable concern for the plight of the person accused of manslaughter. By taking a close look at the biblical concept of asylum we will attempt to glimpse a height of responsibility that is radically foreign to the world we know.

Several of the bodies of legislation in the Hebrew Bible take up the question of the manslayer, who has committed inadvertent homicide, perhaps the result of such mundane occurrences as an errant harvesting blade or a hunting weapon that missed its prey and struck a fellow gamesman.[3] Much like today, people in the ancient period must have been at the wrong end of dropped construction stones, mishandled cutlery, and flying tools. Determining the motive and culpability of the assailant in such tragic situations was as urgent then as it is now. The question of manslaughter and its consequences for justice is interesting enough to warrant sustained attention at both the individual and corporate level. Here we will focus on the responsibility of the community, and in the next chapter we will turn our attention to the question of partial guilt, and the pivotal relationship between intentionality and responsibility.

Hebrew scripture has fairly predictable penalties for the person who is guilty of murder. The desire of ancient peoples to avenge the blood of their fallen kin must have made it difficult for people guilty of manslaughter to escape an unjust execution. In an ideal situation, the killer would wait for a trial where it would be determined whether the killing was intentional. But the anger of grieving families burns hot against the person who caused their grief. The avenger's job was to hunt down the perpetrator for execution. Even if a trial took place and the killing was considered manslaughter, the decision of a judicial body could hardly assuage the grief and anger of a victim's family. Since the blood avenger can act with immunity, the plight of the manslayer is perilous. Scripture attempts to address this problem by providing protection for the manslayer. But who would want to give refuge to someone who *might* be guilty of murder? When the stranger at the door is covered in another person's blood, how inclined are we to open up? The manslayer is on the run, a bloodstained fugitive who may be a murderer.

A cloud of injustice hangs over the situation of manslaughter, as anger and mourning easily translate into rushed judgment and violent resolutions. The easiest solution, of course, is to stay out of the situation, to let violence run its course. But this certainly leaves a substantial loophole in justice. The builder whose hammer slid down a rooftop and killed a passerby is out of luck; blinded by grief and vengeance, grieving relatives can hunt down and kill the careless roofer.[4] Should the fate of the builder be the same as the malicious murderer? Who will ensure that justice happens here, for families and fleeing manslayers?

The laws outlined in Exodus, Numbers, and Deuteronomy are designed to provide protection for the person accused of manslaughter without overlooking responsibility to the families of the victim. Among the biblical answers to manslaughter is the intriguing concept of "cities of asylum," which were places of refuge for bloodstained people awaiting trial as well as extended safe havens for those whose actions were deemed inadvertent. The decision to establish such cities is itself a profound statement of dangerous hospitality. The host city runs great risk to close this loophole in justice.

When a fleeing, bloody-handed person knocks at the door, there are a host of reasons to shut out the fleeing criminal. The chances are decent that the homicide was intentional, and who wants to harbor and protect a murderer? What community wants to risk making itself vulnerable to this kind of danger? The safest solution is surely to leave the door locked and let the manslayer keep running. Certainly, by commonplace understanding of responsibility, this would be justifiable. No cause-and-effect process connects the community to the crime. The lack of this causal connection typically means there is no obligation to help; any finger lifted to help is somehow beyond responsibility and in the realm of charity. But the "city of asylum" makes hospitality mandatory, at least for a few villages. They are responsible to open their doors to hide and protect ambiguously guilty manslayers.

We need not be alarmed at the unreasonable nature of these commandments; it isn't uncommon for commandments in Hebrew scripture to be more prophetic than realistic. There are a few sets of biblical laws and commandments that are so unusual and audacious that scholars doubt Israel ever actually followed the recommendation. The "year of jubilee," for instance, requires that all property be returned to original tribal owners, that servants be set free, and that every debt be forgiven (Lev. 25:11-12, 13-34, 39-54; 27:16-24). These recommendations would seemingly unravel the systems of exchange that make economies thrive. Who would lend someone money the year before the Jubilee? Who would buy land? Most biblical scholars agree that the Jubilee commandments should be read as a hopeful and prophetic dream for a future when individuals and communities are no longer crushed under the constant weight of financial pressure. The very beauty of commandments such as these is the unreasonable, counterintuitive nature of their demands. Their impracticality is instructive; people who aspire to craft a more just world should have these dreams in mind.

On the question of refuge to manslayers we find a set of similarly unreasonable commandments in Exodus, Leviticus, and Numbers. Though an attempt may have been made by Joshua to actually build these cities, it is unlikely they ever functioned in the ways prescribed in Leviticus.[5] However, this has not kept Jewish and Christian scholars from pondering their significance for the practice of justice and hospitality. Among the interesting features of these cities are a lack of formidable walls and an almost complete absence of weapons. This exacerbates the feeling of helplessness such cities must experience; they are not even allowed to arm themselves against the killers who might flee to them to delay their own deaths. In the Jewish Talmud, a set of rabbinical reflections on texts such as these, the rabbis guess the lack of weaponry is intended to prevent the blood avenger from feeling compelled to stop and shop for weapons.[6] Hebrew scripture is so concerned with this small loophole in the system of justice that it demands that entire cities be built with radically different social practices. Entire cities are to be devoted to providing justice for manslayers.

The borders of these cities were to be porous and open. The line between inside and outside the city is marked by standard distances, not barriers, walls, or guards. Residents of such cities must avoid owning rope long enough to be used as a hangman's noose, or any other objects that might attract the eye of an avenger looking for tools of vengeance. These are weapons of revenge, and asylum is to be a place of divine justice.

We encounter again the theme of line drawing and boundary making. In this case, the city has every reasonable right to secure its borders against the dangerous wanderers who might bring mayhem to the community. In chapter 3 we pointed to the subtle and sinister ways that line drawing can consciously and unconsciously lead to oppression and exploitation. But here we find perfectly ordinary lines challenged. The city has every right to protect itself, but the "city of asylum" legislation requires they take responsibility for injustice they did not cause. This cloud of inequity that floats in the air above Israel is to be absorbed by these cities, as they diffuse the violent tension by decreasing their safety and increasing their trepidation. Theirs is a heavy cross to bear, particularly because there is little glory in championing the cause of a bloody-handed killer on the lam.

It is instructive to see how wrenching and countercultural these cities would have been. Among the cornerstones of human religious consciousness is the impulse to be safe and to seek safety through the purity of an inner sanctuary.[7] Mircea Eliade argues that people, ancient and modern, consider their sanctuaries to represent the center of the world.[8] According to a number of ancient cosmological models, the edge of the world is marked by chaos, abysmal waters, horrible monsters, and terrifying danger.[9] Conversely, to be situated at the center of the world, or in the holy sanctuary, is to be the furthest from this chaos and closest to the holiness and stability of the divine. The holy of holies is both a place of great purity and a place of great stability. Israel cannot afford to bring the chaos of the unholy into its holy sanctuary. This would destabilize the established order, inviting chaos into the heart of the world and thereby causing the deity to abandon the sanctuary. But this is exactly what the asylum legislation requires of them. They must open the doors of their city to the chaos of the fugitive and risk exposure to contamination and danger, all for the sake of a potentially innocent fugitive. Much is being asked of these cities and their inhabitants.[10]

As we consider the possibility of being responsible at this extreme level, we cannot help but see a conflict between this issue and Cain's haunting question, "Am I my brother's keeper?" If we are to think seriously about these asylum commandments and their economic parallel in the concept of Ju-bilee, we must move far beyond Cain's assumption that re-sponsibility begins and ends with the self. For citizens of the cities of refuge, the welcoming of dangerous strangers is not optional charity but bedrock responsibility. Their function is to be keepers, and not merely of brothers and sisters, but of anonymous strangers who stumble alarmingly to their door. Cain scoffed at being keeper to his kin; much more is being asked of the residents of the 'arê miqlat (cities of asylum).

What can be learned here about the relationship between responsibility and the clouds of injustice that hang over a bro-ken world? If these laws are more than trivial anecdotes, they surely strain beyond capacity the typical manner in which re-sponsibility is taken. We cannot abide by a definition of re-sponsibility that only addresses the injustice within the field of causation. To be responsible, in this sense, is to take respon-sibility for much more than can be reasonably expected. This theme certainly echoes the sentiment of the laws command-ing extreme hospitality to widows, orphans, and strangers. But here we find the stakes raised, for bloody manslayers do not inspire the same compassion and sympathy. It isn't even just that compassion on manslayers is an unpopular or thank-less endeavor. The city of refuge legislation requires people to do something downright dangerous. They must put their lives at risk for the sake of rectifying an injustice they had no part in causing. The very purpose for the existence of their com-munity is to absorb injustice, owning pain they did not cause.

The unreasonable nature of this level of responsibility is offset by the stark reality that the entrenched models for re-sponsibility simply do not work. Manslaughter is a great exam-ple of a wounding in which the punishment is never commensurate with the crime. The average sentence for manslaughter convictions in the United States is thirty-one months imprisonment.[11] As difficult as it might be to spend almost two and a half years in prison, these lost years can never be compared to the suffering endured by the family of the deceased or the lost potential of a life that should not yet be over. There is a cloud of injustice that hangs over the situation, even after all accounts have been legally settled.

The pain that remains after restitution is not particular to the crime of manslaughter but lingers in countless ways in even the smallest of infractions. The difference between crime and punishment can run the other direction as well. Artists often depict justice as a blindfolded woman holding a scale, attempting to weigh matters objectively and make equitable rulings. But in matters of pain and suffering, objectivity and equity are elusive, if not impossible to attain. We are stuck with the residue of past injustice, no matter how sincerely those before us struggled to do the right thing.

This residue is also noticed and addressed in the "cities of refuge" legislation. If the defendant is found guilty of manslaughter, but not murder, he or she is not free to go. The city of refuge is also designed to absorb the residue of anger and injustice that remains even after a fair trial. The manslayer is sent back to the city of refuge after being convicted of manslaughter, to live in exile until the family's anger subsides.[12] If the slayer leaves the boundaries of the city, he or she is fair game for the blood avenger to kill with immunity. The place of asylum is also a place of confinement. The role of these communities was to deter the crimes of passion that might follow the loss of life. But they were also being called to absorb the residual unrest that can never be assuaged by any verdict.

This is a high version of responsibility, a daunting and overwhelming prospect. How do modern communities perform such extreme acts of hospitality? It seems compelling to consider that the great clouds of injustice that hang over the world today are waiting for communities to take responsibility for them. Any organization, Christian or otherwise, that wishes to address a world full of injustice must quit confining the concept of responsibility to the realm of cause and effect. If the asylum legislation teaches us anything, it is that someone must take responsibility for unclaimed pain, tension, and suffering. I suspect that these fascinating laws provide a glimpse of the way communities of justice must function. In a world full of unclaimed suffering, what we need are *'arê miqlat*— communities of refuge. We must *be* asylum.

In Jesus' Good Samaritan parable, mentioned in chapter 3, the true neighbor is the one who pays the debt he does not owe. Jesus tells that story in response to a question given to him by an inquisitive lawyer who comes seeking "eternal life," much like the young ruler discussed in chapter 1. The man repeats Jesus' familiar, twofold summary of the law: to love God with all your heart, soul, strength, and mind and to love "your neighbor as yourself" (Luke 10:27). then he pushes Jesus by asking, "And who is my neighbor?" Rather than answer him directly, Jesus tells the story of the Good Samaritan.

Of interest here is the insinuation that the Good Samaritan has not performed some sort of extraordinary act of charity, but the basic and most fundamental requirement of the law. The man from Samaria is just *being responsible* when he takes care of the beaten traveler. And this places the bar of responsibility frighteningly high.

Violence is circular. Collateral damage is inevitable when bombs are dropped and wars are waged. People who have no investment in the conflict will suffer, and their suffering will produce anger and incline them to violence. Even when violence succeeds in its aim to bring about some brand of justice, a cloud of bitterness and resentment hangs in the air. Remarkably, these asylum laws prescribe a kind of absorption of violence that does not participate in the circle of revenge. These commandments proclaim that the backbone of the law is justice, not revenge. The pursuit of justice requires people and communities who are willing to sacrifice for a future that cannot come to pass if every person seeks to minimize responsibility, investment, risk, and suffering.

Like the cities of refuge, Christian communities committed to being responsible must lay down the line-drawing mechanism that might make the churches forbidding and hostile places for people who suffer. Judgmental rhetoric and attitudes serve to alienate the outsider. No wall holds the stranger at a distance more effectively than a harsh and judgmental atmosphere. The sharp lines often drawn between the church and the world can also create a kind of insulation from responsibility. But hostility is a form of irresponsibility. Put simply, the floating, unclaimed injustice that plagues the world today *is the responsibility of the church*. The causal connection between the church, the Christian, and the suffering experienced by others is irrelevant to the question of responsibility. I am responsible for the suffering of the other, even if I did not cause the suffering.

We are moving our way steadily toward a practical and philosophical quandary. How is it possible to be *this* responsible? Are the claims being made here so unreasonable that they are irrelevant? For now we can see that a certain measure of unrest is necessary for genuine Christianity and authentic human life. To be committed to justice and responsibility is to fix one's attention beyond the confines of one's own actions and their consequences. I am responsible for a future that stands in an impossible relation to the present. The cessation of poverty is seemingly impossible, as is the end of war, oppression, bigotry, and exploitation. Living toward that goal requires a particular kind of faith, a faith in the impossible. To be more precise, it requires that one operate on a logic that makes little sense in the present. This level of hospitality remains absurd by any present measure. Providing asylum to wandering murderers only makes sense according to the counterintuitive logic of a future only glimpsed as radical hope.

In *The Fugitive*, Dr. Kimble looks very guilty. A 911 call placed by his wife seems to implicate him, along with a number of other pieces of evidence used to condemn him to death. He finds very few people to help him in his struggle for justice. The biblical commandment to build cities of refuge seems to indicate that the church ought to be a community that bends and contorts itself to be a home for people caught under the vice of hasty judgment. Such hospitality certainly implies the risk that the church will provide asylum for *guilty* runners as well. It will surely be the case that senseless acts of compassion, forgiveness, and sacrifice will look completely unreasonable. But who guaranteed that responsibility would be reasonable?

six

INTENTION'S ROAD

THE 2008 SUMMER OLYMPICS in Beijing was the most watched television event in history. Athletes from obscure sports that rarely got international attention had their events broadcast around the world for all to see. Among the athletes who might wish NBC had occasionally averted the cameras is Cuban taekwondo champion Angel Matos. Taekwondo is a rough sport, and injuries are not unusual. Olympic rules allow taekwondo athletes to take a maximum injury time-out of one minute. Matos was injured in the bronze-medal match, which he was leading, after his foot crashed into the leg of his opponent. The match was stopped for Matos to recover, but his minute expired before he could receive medical attention. The referee then ended the bout, awarding the victory and the bronze medal to Kazakhstan's Arman Chilmanov. Matos was not pleased. When pleading with the referee made no headway, Matos lost his temper. He wheeled around and kicked the referee squarely in the face.

Athletes throw their share of tantrums. They are rarely elevated to high public esteem because of their composure and poise. What is unusual and fascinating about this particular incident is the penalty handed down by the International Olympic Committee (IOC). Almost immediately after the incident, Matos was banned for life from Olympic competition. He is unlikely to ever again participate in international taekwondo competitions. But this penalty is to be expected. What is surprising is that the IOC also handed down a lifetime ban to *his coach*.

I have had the honor of coaching teams from a variety of sports, and there have been many moments when I hung my head in shame at the behavior of "my" athletes on the gym floor, soccer field, baseball diamond, or wrestling mat. No matter how many hours you spend grinding the ideals of fair play and sportsmanship into the minds of children and teenagers, the messages of a coach always compete with a host of other forces. In the complicated world of childhood and adolescence, and surely adulthood as well, the complexities of life spill onto the field of play. Tempers flare and tears fall. I've seen players strip down to their underwear, flop on the court and refuse to move, scream profanities, shove referees, and throw punches. I am rather relieved I was not held responsible for their behavior.

Leudis Gonzalez, the man who coached Matos, was less fortunate. His penalty was exactly as severe as the athlete he trained. Should a coach be responsible for the behavior of his or her players? The IOC clearly pins shared guilt on the athlete and the coach. The equal penalties indicate equal responsibility. But is this *fair*? Should parents be responsible for the behavior of their children? Teachers for the failures of their pupils? Pastors and priests for the sins of their flock? In many cases we can see no indication that these people deserve to be held liable for the behavior of their athletes, students, and children. No pastor or priest can be effective enough to prevent some parishioner from acting irresponsibly. Parents often shake their head in disbelief at the behavior of their children, wondering, "Where did we go wrong?"

College football coach Gary Barnett was beset by scandals during his tenure at the University of Colorado. A steady stream of at least eight women accused Colorado football players of rape. As one scandalous accusation piled on top of another, Barnett was pinned down by the media to discuss whether he was at all responsible for the behavior of his players. He tried to claim some responsibility for both on-field and off-field behavior but claimed there are significant limitations to how a coach can influence a player. "I have 48 [players] that I have held accountable over the last five years," he told a panel investigating his role in the scandals. "I can't live their lives for them."[1] Under closer examination it was discovered that Barnett's recruiters had lured potential players with drugs, alcohol, and sex.[2] The *New York Times* pointed out that the university was not sufficiently embarrassed by these episodes to fire Barnett.[3] It took a losing season of football to warrant his dismissal.

Certainly the coaches in these instances did not *intend* for their players to kick referees and commit rape. In courts, responsibility is often tied to intentionality, which is why Barnett was not fired for the irresponsible behavior of his players and recruiters. The coach, apparently, meant well. Gonzalez was banned from Olympic taekwondo for life, though he threw no punch and kicked no face. We have an interesting contrast in ethics at work here, a profound question about shared accountability. The question of intentionality runs to the heart of responsibility, since legal interpretations of responsibility regularly hinge on the question of intention. This coincides with religious considerations; many theological positions consider people responsible for their actions only if the behavior was intentionally malicious. The best excuse in the world, apparently, is, "I didn't mean to do it."

This is one of the most obvious aspects of the default understanding of responsibility in North America. To be responsible is not only to be at fault but also to *be aware* that one's actions are causing someone suffering. This provides a stunning loophole for evasion, a ring of Gyges to avoid being responsible for one's actions. The impulse to discern who is at fault when things go wrong is legitimate and valid; it is even necessary for the courts, for reparations, and sometimes for the important work of reconciliation. At the same time, the fault-finding investigations that determine liability may not be as relevant to Christian responsibility as we often presume. Even when blame cannot be avoided, the question of intentionality remains. Countless not-guilty verdicts have been delivered because the prosecution failed to "show intent." Coaches, parents, pastors, and priests mostly mean well. The point is not that they should be found guilty or accused of anything. For Christians, the scandal is a summons to take responsibility even when no one can justifiably place it on their heads.

In the Talmud, the discussion of manslaughter gives significant consideration to the responsibilities of the "coach." As the rabbis contemplate the importance of the Deut. 4 asylum laws, a question is raised about the culpability of a rabbi when one of his students commits a crime like manslaughter. If a student kills accidentally and must flee to a city of refuge, the student's teacher must accompany the pupil into exile.[4] The master is not just responsible for his own welfare, but for that of his pupil as well. The ancient Israelite conception of sin, intentional or otherwise, is primarily social and therefore not individualistic. This means the master and the pupil are bound together in liability for actions, intentional or otherwise. The difference between this perspective on responsibility and our default understanding is stark. The penalty given Gonzalez by the IOC makes perfect sense to some people and seems remarkably harsh and strange to others. The difference illustrates widely varying models of responsibility.

The instruction that passes between teacher and student is primarily about *vigilance*. Education is training in awareness, the opening of one's eyes to the scope of issues to be addressed in the world. By this logic, bad education is anything that closes down our perspective on responsibility. Poor teaching makes students less aware, less awake, less inclined to see the connections between their lives and the world that confronts them. The teacher who fails to guide a student into responsible behavior shares in the damages caused by the careless student.

It should be noted that for the rabbinic tradition, students are carefully chosen for religious instruction. Part of the rabbi's culpability stems from the fact that he chose his students. A common dictum declared: "Let no one teach the Torah to a disciple that is unworthy."[5] The analogy to modern teaching and coaching is therefore not perfect. Our professors, coaches, and teachers do not usually have the option of dropping students and athletes. Still, I do not think this means that the analogy fails entirely. A surprising degree of responsibility appears in every opportunity to lead, educate, parent, or coach.

The decision of the IOC to ban Leudis Gonzalez for life is perfectly consistent with the Talmudic reflections on manslaughter. The coach is responsible for the actions of the student. Like the rabbis teaching the wisdom of Scripture, Gonzalez should have trained his pupil more responsibly. This level of responsibility, which surely extends in some degree to a host of relationships, is uncomfortable at several different levels. To claim I am responsible for the actions of my students is to find that the extent of my responsibility is outside of my control. As hard as I work to train and instruct my children, students, or employees, their behavior rests in their own hands. We should shudder at the thought that we might be held to this great height of responsibility. Our pupils and staff will surely act in ways we do not intend, but good intentions do not bring the dead back to life. Good intentions may exonerate in court, but they do little to address the cloud of injustice that hovers wherever there is suffering. Perhaps the common quip is truer than we realize: "The road to hell is paved with good intentions."

The issue of manslaughter pushes this very question; it is only *intent* that differentiates manslaughter from murder. It is worthwhile to note that the Hebrew word for manslayer is the same as that for murderer. The *rotseach* (murderer) is guilty, by either accident or intention. One might argue, then, that the delineation in these texts is between *types* of sin and the variety of consequences one must suffer for sinning.[6] That the *rotseach* is guilty is unquestioned; the degree of intentionality is important only in determining the severity of the punishment. A lack of intentionality is therefore not enough in the Torah or the Talmud to escape guilt.

For the legislation in Leviticus, full innocence is not a consideration when someone has died. The murder is either accidental or intentional. The suffering is indisputable; an innocent person is dead, and a family mourns the senseless loss of a loved one. With more caution and care, and perhaps less concern for expedience and profit, the hammer would still be in the roofer's hand and the loved one still living. There is a difference, clearly, between the two sins. One merits a different penalty than the other, but they are sins nonetheless.

The distinction between intentional and unintentional sin is carefully analyzed by eighteenth-century theologian John Wesley. Acts committed without "will" or "unholy desire" are labeled "infirmities" and, according to Wesley, should not be considered sin.[7] Elsewhere Wesley calls them "sins improperly so-called," characterized by "involuntary transgression of divine law, known or unknown."[8] Wesley's concern is to affirm that a person truly redeemed is freed by grace from the power of sin. If even the unintentional infractions are considered sin, how could anyone ever be free of sinfulness? This desire to differentiate between intentional sins and unintentional "mistakes" is designed to ease the concerns of earnest Christians who are struggling to align their lives with the way of life Wesley called Christian perfection.

But does Wesley's zeal to emphasize liberation from sin leave his followers blind to the partial guilt of the careless roofer? Wesley carefully acknowledges that both forms of sin require atonement, but he insists that only one sort of transgression properly qualifies for the definition of "sin." To sin, argues Wesley, one must know and will one's wrongdoing.

It would be unfair to accuse Wesley of turning a blind eye to sins of ignorance or omission; John Wesley's life is a testament to his commitment to the poor, the sick, and London's oppressed working class. But I am less concerned here with Wesley's legacy than I am about the consequences of his decision to differentiate between willful and accidental transgressions. By rendering only intentional acts as qualified for the title "sin," Wesley helps widen a loophole that makes possible a tremendous amount of unclaimed damages. Bodies and lives and communities suffer, but nobody "meant" to hurt anyone. Whatever Wesley's noble intentions for limiting the definition of sin, I fear that the result of this delineation is a perceptible shift away from the sort of extreme responsibility advocated in these biblical texts.

In the biblical and Talmudic interpretations of the cities of asylum, these refuge places are both asylum from the avenger and a form of house arrest. The killer residing in one of these cities is banished into exile, both protected and punished. For the murderer, there is conviction and capital punishment. But the manslayer, though found innocent of murder, still has bloody hands. He cannot go back to his roof and continue to swing his hammer. He remains guilty, neither fully absolved nor fully condemned.

The implication is that unintentional sin is quite effective in breeding intentional sin. Falling hammers produce hearts inflamed with rage, a rage that the Bible clearly condones and for which considerable allowance is made. But the pain experienced in suffering and loss is not fully erased by any juridical decision. Residue remains; a remainder of suffering that can easily lead to more injustice, revenge piled on revenge. The cities of refuge are thus both compassionate and just, addressing both the crime and the residue. These are places of both safe asylum and just punishment for unintentional sin.

What the Talmud realizes, and what perhaps escapes the "willful transgression" motif of Wesley's understanding of sin, is that in a world where there is suffering and victimization, responsibility is not so easily bound by lines of individual or momentary intention. We may ask, "How can we glean from the fertile concept of asylum a more robust concept of responsibility?"

There is something deeply unsettling about the implications of being responsible for damages we did not intend. Philosopher Emmanuel Levinas claims we often act in a fog or "twilight."[9] We are aware and unaware, awake and drowsy, to the consequences and implications of our actions. For this haze, contends Levinas, we are responsible. Because we cannot ever become fully awake or aware of our responsibilities, we are never vigilant enough. It is possible that we share more in common with the manslayer and the blood avenger than we might wish to admit. We fume in rage over injustices that cause us suffering, often ignorant of the fires we light behind us.

Perhaps Wesley's practical and sermonic division between intentional sin and unintentional transgression has served its purpose and run its course. Wesley would have loathed the idea of Christians retreating behind the facade of unintentionality. However benevolent his intentions were for this delineation, it leaves us vulnerable to the ravages of individualism. The loophole is obvious; sin is a category of will and intentionality, and we can quite unintentionally wreak havoc on the world. In his reflections on the Talmud, Levinas shows repeatedly that the wisdom of biblical asylum texts is their persistent subversion of any attempt to delineate where responsibility begins and ends. Though penalties and levels of guilt vary, the biblical legislators consistently resist the impulse to draw a line to delineate where "sin" starts and stops.

According to Levinas, the "anthropology of the West" considers the foundation of human nature to be the autonomous and thinking self.[10] The form of morality produced by this emphasis is heavy on the line drawing that determines the extent of personal obligations. One must first understand where responsibility begins and ends before assessing the moral rectitude of an individual. But the Torah is more interested in *just societies* than the moral status of the individual. This is why the Torah resists the reduction of responsibility to the extent of actions one *intends*. The asylum legislation and the concept of manslaughter illustrate the slippery nature of ancient Hebrew ethics. Responsibility is not easily pinned down; it moves around the lines we draw in the sand and lays claim to a level of obligation that is offensive and even dangerous. I believe the Talmud and the New Testament commonly repeat and extend the extreme level of hospitality offered in the pages of the Torah.

The form of anthropology I am advocating here is a reversal of the Western understanding of selfhood and responsibility. We are taught that "be true to yourself" precedes our obligations to others. I am claiming that *responsibility is the fundamental property of human existence*. Ethics thus precedes all philosophy. To be human is to be a respondent, a person asymmetrically inclined to the other who has already spoken, called, and required. The impulse to limit the scope of responsibility is itself an impulse to limit the voice and call of God, most audible in the suffering face of the human other.

When we slow down the frames of the asylum process, we discover that responsibility itself is an evasive but central aspect to reality. Responsibility moves like uncontainable wind across our communities. The impulse to say, "It was not my fault" or "I am not responsible for those damages," is an inhumane or antihuman urge. The specter of Cain rises again, asking the haunting question, "Am I my brother's keeper?" Just how vigilant must I be?

A final lesson from the Torah solidifies this understanding of extreme responsibility. In the book of Exodus an interesting problem is addressed about fires and their danger. No matter how carefully one tends a fire, the chance always exists that an ember will escape and burn down houses and fields. Exodus 22:6 reads, "When a fire breaks out and catches in thorns so that the stacked grain or the standing grain or the field is consumed, the one who started the fire shall make full restitution." In the Torah, here, and in many other places, intentionality is not the primary concern. The chief concern is on the suffering caused by the accident. What matters most is alleviating the suffering, addressing the cloud of injustice that hangs dark over the family whose fields are scorched and barren. Is it fair to expect a vigilant fire-lighter to pay for damages caused by bad luck and foul winds? Hardly. But contrary to popular understandings of ethics, responsibility is not about fairness. Biblical morality elevates suffering to a higher level of importance than fairness; the playing field is not supposed to be level. The widow, the poor, the orphan, and the oppressed are owed more than we can be fairly expected to offer. Responsibility is thus not tied to what can be expected of the self but to the suffering of the world.

We light fires constantly and innocently enough, with words and deeds that have both positive and negative influence on those who live around us and around the world. The wind blows our embers in places we never *intend* them to go. Who hasn't delivered a well-intended compliment only to discover it was received as an insult?

How often do we acknowledge our responsibility for the damages wrought by our fires? With the wrong sorts of winds, or with the slightest bit of carelessness, the most innocent of words or deeds could therefore do deep and permanent damage. Perhaps a careless comment about a young girl's lunch contributes to an eating disorder; a dismissive look reinforces a young man's depression; a distracted yawn convinces a friend that you don't care about her story. Even extreme caution cannot prevent fires from breaking out, small and large, in the wake of our actions. For these fires, it seems, we are responsible. Gonzalez is responsible for his violent athlete. I am responsible for the actions of my children, my students, my friends, and my college.

The world of athletics holds more than just negative examples of responsibility. The Internet has immortalized the shocking hospitality of a few softball players from Central Washington. Sara Tucholsky, a seldom-used outfielder playing her senior season for Western Oregon stepped to the plate on an otherwise ordinary April day. In what would be the final swing of her college career, Tucholsky connected for a game-changing home run, the first of her life. But in her excitement and surprise she missed first base and had to turn around to make sure she stepped on the bag. As she turned her right knee collapsed, leaving her in a heap in the dirt. She would have to crawl back to first base to get credited with a single.

If a teammate or coach touched her, she'd be out. In a move Gary Hays of ESPN calls "the ultimate act of sportsmanship," two players on the opposing team picked up Tucholsky and carried her around the bases, gently lowering her body to touch each one.[11] Mallory Holtman, the Central Washington fielder who came up with the idea to carry Tucholsky around the bases, humbly deflected the praise for her tear-jerking actions. Swamped by interviewers and attention afterward, she consistently downplayed her actions. "Granted I thought of it, but everyone else would have done it. . . . it shows what our program is all about and what kind of people we have here."

Pam Knox, the Western Oregon coach who watched her little outfielder being carried around the bases, was floored. "It was such a lesson that we learned—that it is not all about winning. . . . as coaches, we're always trying to get to the top . . . but I will never, ever forget this moment. It's changed me, and I'm sure it's changed my players." The hospitality and responsibility of the Central Washington players rattles free of all the logical and prescribed ways that "sportsmanship" is expected to function. This story is a marvel because it interrupts all expectations with an event that is radically different from its surroundings. This is a *holy* moment.

Athletic competition provides obvious lines, rules, and boundaries that make vivid the unusual choices of athletes. But away from the fields there is an abundance of pain much less visible than Tucholsky's knee. By no fault of our own, we wake up to a world full of pain. Responsibility viewed through the lens of Jewish and Christian scriptures is not a product of internal moral obligations. Responsibility arises from the need of the other, from the pain of those who suffer. The Western world has tended to bind responsibility to a sense of what can be fairly asked of any given person. The model of responsibility on display in the Bible can be contrasted sharply to this default manner of gauging the responsibility of individual persons. We are not only responsible for damages we did not cause and the damages we did not intend to cause but also for suffering to which we cannot be connected.

We are all manslayers, at best, fire-lighters who only sometimes see how hot and hurtful our flames burn. The question that remains is simple: "How can we live under the weight of responsibility this great?" It is to this question that we now turn our direct attention.

seven

HAKELDEMA: A TALE OF TWO FIELDS

IT IS A LONELY SCENE, really. Knowing that he has just set up the immanent crucifixion of Jesus, Judas stumbles his way back to the place of his most egregious transgression. Only the gospel of Matthew bothers to report evidence of a major reversal in Judas's mentality between the Gethsemane betrayal and his suicide by hanging. We learn in Matt. 27 that Judas has something of a change of heart when he hears that Jesus will soon die because of Judas's actions. While his original motives are unrecoverable, Matthew carefully notes that Judas "repented"[1] and retraced his steps, silver in hand, to the religious leaders who were behind the conspiracy against Jesus (v. 3). Judas appeals to these men by offering the sweet sound of a specific and heartfelt confession. "I have sinned," he claims (v. 4a). But these priests will offer him no avenue of absolution. Appealing to the faces of religious authority, Judas is turned away with these stunning words of priestly failure: "What is that to us? See to it yourself" (v. 4b).[2]

As we turn our attention toward what can be done about the cloud of injustice that hangs over the world, it is important to address the phenomenon of suffering and how it multiplies. We have practical examples at our disposal; people who have been wounded are more likely to wound others. Abusers are more likely to abuse. Victims of racial violence are more likely to commit acts of racial violence. The cycle is vicious and seemingly endless.

We have no shortage of stories of suffering in Christian and Jewish scripture; human suffering laces almost every chapter in the Bible and nearly every page of human history. We will focus on two such stories of suffering in this chapter, two stories bound together by the simple act of "purchasing a field." The brand of daring hope I am advocating in this book will be evident in one purchase and starkly missing in the other. The story of Judas affords us with an opportunity to analyze one instance of lonely suffering and its result. For Judas, this includes his trip to the temple in remorse, his lonely suicide, and the haunting field that becomes his graveyard. The story of Judas provides a disturbing snapshot of missed responsibility. At the same time, this narrative begins to bring into focus what must be done to prevent the spiral of injustice and violence. After dwelling on Judas, we will briefly turn our attention to the unusual and hopeful purchase of a field by the Hebrew prophet Jeremiah.

It is not the death of Jesus but the shocking indifference of the priests' words that immediately precipitates Judas's suicide. In one stunning verse Matthew describes Judas's reaction to this cold response: "Throwing down the pieces of silver in the temple, he departed; and he went and hanged himself" (27:5). Why does Matthew pause to tell us this part of the story? A quick look at the other three gospels indicates that Matthew had a unique perspective on Judas and his demise. John and Luke have a particularly negative perspective on Judas, chalking his actions up to those of a man possessed. The gospel of Matthew seems to befriend Judas, to a degree, or at least to sympathize with his plight after the coins hit his pocket. When the author of Luke and Acts pauses to mention Judas again in Acts 1, the narrative is parenthetical and violent. Judas dashes himself to pieces in a barren and empty field (vv. 18-20).

Matthew includes the remorseful journey back to the priests, and Judas's lonely trek to his suicidal tree. In a book about responsibility, we may legitimately ponder: "How responsible is Judas for the death of Jesus? How culpable?" He certainly moves to a swift and effective self-execution in response to his guiltiness. But before he does so, he goes looking for help. He finds the opposite. In most retellings of Christianity's central story, Judas plays the classic scapegoat. He is the "bad guy," whose character can absorb the anger and aggression produced by the story of Jesus' crucifixion. In Luke's mind, and certainly John's, the actions of Judas are literally satanic.[3] But by Matthew's telling, Judas is confused and remorseful and perhaps shocked that his actions have led to Jesus' death sentence. If Judas is like the wandering manslayer, he finds no refuge in the sanctuary of the priests.

Judas, in a denial that mirrors Peter's, is not convinced at the Last Supper that he is the foretold betrayer. He does not believe that the horrible and damning passage quoted by Jesus can really apply to him and his Passover scheme: "Surely not I, Rabbi?" (Matt. 26:23-25).[4] The motivations and emotions behind Judas's betrayal escape even the most careful readings of these texts, but he is clearly presented by Matthew as an ambivalent character. Judas denies being the prophesied betrayer, dips his hand into the bowl with Jesus, kisses Jesus at the moment of betrayal, is profoundly anguished when Jesus is condemned, repents anxiously, and ultimately commits suicide.[5] This is an erratic and perplexing pattern of behavior; Judas is more complex than we often give him credit for being.

A fascinating element of the Judas narrative is the "Field of Blood" that is purchased with the money Judas gained from betraying Jesus (27:8). Judas dumps his money on the temple floor in disgust and immediately leaves to commit suicide. The priests and elders are unsure about what should be done with this money. It was once theirs, but now it has been tainted. It is marked by sin, ill-gotten and ill-fated. Sensitive to the laws in Deuteronomy that forbid donations of money gained through sinful means,[6] the priests are stuck with a pile of money that cannot simply be added to the temple coffers. For the priests to accept this money would connect the sacred with the sinful. This money had to be used for profane, or at least mundane, purposes. Their inventive solution is clever indeed. They choose a practical and religiously correct use for the money.[7] Judas's blood money is used to purchase a blood field, given the Aramaic name *Hakeldema*, a profane place if ever there was one.[8] Literally translated, *Hakeldema* means "field of blood." This will be the place of faceless burials and nameless graves, a cemetery for foreigners. Judas's money purchases a graveyard not worthy of even the lowliest of Israelites. Today, the place traditionally attributed to Judas's graveyard is a garbage dump.

To understand the significance of this field it is worth spending a few minutes exploring the significance of graveyards in ancient Israel. A longstanding respect and concern over places of burial is apparent in even the earliest Hebrew religious experience. Long before a subjective afterlife is a consideration, Abraham, Isaac, and Jacob are profoundly concerned about where they will be buried. With ceremony it is reported that in dying and being buried Abraham "was gathered to his people" (Gen. 25:8). The same phrase is repeated upon Isaac's death, his passage out of life and into sacred burial is a movement into "his people" (35:29). Jacob died insisting that his remains be carried out of Egypt; he did not wish for his body to reside in a foreign land, no matter how friendly and inviting the Egyptians might seem. "I am about to be gathered to my people," said Jacob, sensing his immanent death. "Bury me with my ancestors—in the cave . . . that Abraham bought. . . . There Abraham and his wife Sarah were buried; there Isaac and his wife Rebekah were buried; and there I buried Leah" (49:29-31). David "slept with his ancestors," as did his son Solomon (1 Kings 2:10; 11:43). To die and be buried in exile, or even worse to lie unburied on the ground, is a great terror to the ancient Israelite. To imagine one's bones lying blanched and unburied in a field forever is an ultimate nightmare of restless torment. For these people, to be denied the "rest" of a proper burial was to be cursed to an eternity of wandering and loneliness, a permanent banishment. "Hell" is being eaten by vultures.

Burial is about *rest*, and in the culture of ancient Israel the final act of hospitality and responsibility is to bury people respectfully and permanently. We would not be exaggerating to suppose that the most profane locations would be the places where nameless foreigners are buried. Even Jewish criminals deserved better than to be buried in Judas's nightmarish

Hakeldema. The name "field of blood" leaves images of lasting bloodstains on this land. But this place is bloody in a different manner than an old battlefield, where violent death takes its place in a broader spectrum of meaning. Soldiers die nobly, at least sometimes; casualties of war die in defense of land and family or perhaps in trying to seize new territory. But a foreigner's death happens far from family and historical burial grounds. No one remains to carry corpses to sacred tombs or provide a proper funeral. Judas's legacy is a sad, empty, restless, and profane graveyard.

Hakeldema is the wasteland of broken and forgotten meaning; it is an alien, bloody, monstrous place devoid of comfort and familiarity. This word epitomizes solitude and separation from the community. Integral to understanding spatial *Hakeldema* is the temporal element to this haunting place. Corpses are not only in a place but also in a *time* of interminable suspension and everlasting restlessness. It is a terrifying thing to move into a place of lonely despair, but the real terror arises from the sense that the cloud of despair will never lift. Judas's suicide fits well here; his suicide note is the pile of money tossed at the feet of the priests. He dies, not because he has done something despicable, but because he cannot conceive of a future worth living. His despair is permanent. The field becomes a graveyard where even in death foreigners are eternally damned to be weary and lonesome wanderers. *Hakeldema* is what happens to the abandoned, forlorn, and suffering faces of our world. Judas went to his death without much fanfare. Others wander the earth as lost souls, leaving shattered lives and damaged communities in their wake. Wounded, broken people do a tremendous amount of wounding and breaking.

It hardly seems a stretch to use this word *Hakeldema* to represent the loneliness, suffering, and despair produced by the unclaimed injustices of the world. People who dwell in this lonely land are also likely to be desperate, suspicious, angry, biased, and defensive. When we enter such a state of lonely despair, we are severed from the community of faces that holds us fast. In *Hakeldema* nobody trusts anyone; the bloodstained ground is a constant reminder to keep one's guard up, to lock tight the doors, and secure ourselves against the dangers of the strange, the different, and the unknown. The world we live in can sometimes look very much like Judas's blood field.

Hakeldema is like the home of Gollum in Tolkien's *Lord of the Rings*. Gollum lived in a small island in the middle of a dark underground lake, far beneath a looming mountain. His existence was pitiful and insular; he knew no society. When people, hobbits, or goblins appeared at the shore of his icy, underground pond, he saw them as either food or threat. Tolkien provides little detail about Gollum's ancient past, but he was apparently driven from the society of his youth and fled underground. The darkness and loneliness of his cold home, coupled with the internal world produced by the magic ring he found, left him to haunt the underworld. This lonely, restless existence contorted his body and soul until he became incapable of healthy relationships. Judas is also driven away, by the cold words of the priests and the indifference of his friends. He doesn't stick around to hurt anyone else.

Judas is failed in at least two ways following his change of heart, first by the priests from whom he seeks absolution and second by the community of disciples that fails to situate themselves between Judas's despair and his suicidal trip into *Hakeldema*. In both cases Judas is left *alone* to deal with his despair. The starkest denial of community comes at the hands of the priest. They may, in fact, have delivered a message to Judas that is a deeper cause for despair than even his ghastly betrayal of Jesus. Judas comes refunding the blood money he had received for betraying Jesus, and his request for absolution is not entirely unreasonable. He does not come to the priests asking that they find a way to reverse his sin and turn Jesus loose. By appearing again at the temple Judas is confronting the terror of his private despair. For help in this confrontation he turns to the faces of the priests. Their response to Judas is nothing short of a death sentence. Seeking forgiveness and confessing to these religious leaders, Judas hears in reply: "What is that to us? See to it yourself" (Matt. 27:4).

If Judas is to find forgiveness, he is told to look for it within the context of his own life, amid the rubble of his private emptiness and self-loathing. He must move on alone, with no face of love to call him out of a fixation on his despicable failure. Judas came to the priests to save his life, perhaps as a final attempt to rescue a future, however bleak. But Judas is turned away by the coldest and most heartless words of Matthew's gospel. Do you seek a future for your broken, guilty life? "See to it yourself." Are you dwelling in that dark and silent place where there is truly no hope in sight? "What is that to us?" Are there any crueler words in all of Christian scripture? Judas is lost in private desolation and his religious guides turn his sorrow back upon itself, perhaps redoubling his loneliness and desperation. We need not even stretch this text to see the connection between the response of the priests and Judas's suicide. They are linked inextricably. The blood of Judas stains the hands of the priests who refused to honor the sanctity of their religious responsibilities. The priests turned an opportunity for healing into *Hakeldema*; they refused to raise even a finger of hospitality to Judas's sincere request for absolution. By turning his anguish over to the priests, Judas was offering his pain up to be embraced and addressed by others. They refused.

The second way in which Judas is failed is more subtle, but perhaps even more instructive for Christian communities today. Where are Judas's friends in his darkest hour? His walk to *Hakeldema* is a walk (perhaps run) of existential despair. Suicide is a lonely and solitary act, and despite our inability to access Judas's private pain and personal crisis we should not look past the experience of this individual. In the face of Jesus' crucifixion, the fractured community of disciples fails to take account of their missing brother. One can speculate that they are perhaps angry with Judas, spiteful at his betrayal, and now consider him to be a dangerous alien, a monstrosity, an outsider. Peter and the other scattered disciples (except perhaps the faithful women who follow Jesus all the way to the tomb) appear to be caught up in their own disappointments and failures. They are too absorbed to stand between Judas and his noose. Some of them may have clung together after Jesus died, but do any of them give a second thought about Judas? Is his sin beyond the reach of their forgiveness? We can only wonder.

It is fair to side with the disciples on this one; how can they be expected to care about Judas or try to prevent whatever form of self-punishment he might administer? The disciples ignore their repentant and sorrowful brother, perhaps ignorant of his remorse. Like the priest and elders, Judas's friends fail him miserably, but they can justifiably claim that Judas dug his own grave. Yet his suicide happens because no one has offered him a future, no rest from the pressure of guilt and self-loathing, no respite for his lonely and solitary despair. The communal pathways to forgiveness and life have been sealed off; he has been told to seek his own redemption, and the chasm of despair opens up beneath him. Without the priests, without his friends, Judas chooses the lonely and sad suicidal fate. No face stands between Judas and his *Hakeldema*. No Eucharistic bread or wine is extended to a man starving for lack of a future. To Judas the table is closed.

Only a scandalous articulation of responsibility would dare to question the obligation of the disciples for the death of Judas. Of course Judas is unlikely to have left a trail for them to follow, even if they had tried to find him. In stark contrast, freshman Rutgers student Tyler Clementi posted a Facebook status update announcing his intentions to commit suicide after his roommate streamed live footage of a homosexual encounter on the Internet. He wrote, "Jumping off the [George Washington] bridge sorry."[9] Unlike Judas, Clementi let all of his friends know where he planned to commit suicide and when—September 22, 2010, 8:42 p.m. We should be out looking for Tyler. He is *my* responsibility. We pushed him to his *Hakeldema* and left him to jump like Judas, alone. And children like Tyler will continue to find their way to the George Washington Bridge until we embrace our responsibility for the pain they carry.

If *Hakeldema* is a lonely, bloody graveyard, the community of early Christians should have been the opposite. Instead, they were scattered and isolated in their disappointment and despair. In contrast to the restlessness of the wandering sufferer, the community should offer *Sabbath*, restful peace. Much attention is given to the concept and practice of Sabbath observance in the Hebrew Bible, the Talmud, and the Christian New Testament. The seeds of the concept are found in a few short lines on the tablets of the Ten Commandments (see Exod. 20:8-11). Here, in its most abbreviated form, after requiring rest for children, slaves, and livestock, the commandment reaches an even more astounding point. Even aliens are to be given rest on this day. Aliens were at this point in Israel's history, by definition, foreign to the worship of Yahweh. The sanctity of Saturday apparently knows no exemption. All Sabbath rest is holy. Sabbath opposes *Hakeldema*, where bodies and souls dwell in endless unrest. Israel is to provide a hospitable setting for Saturday rest, even to those hostile to the worship of Yahweh. Children, slaves, livestock, and foreigners are at the mercy of the community. They are only given rest when a space and time are created for such *shalom*. The failure to provide space for Sabbath peace is a fundamental failure of responsibility. There can be no places of banishment outside of the reach of this holy day; *Hakeldema* is Sabbath violation. This irrational and other-centered hospitality is the marker of Sabbath observance.

The purchase of *Hakeldema* is reminiscent of the story of Jeremiah's rather irrational purchase of a potter's field.[10] Facing the impending doom of invasion, Jeremiah foolishly spends money to buy property that is likely to be soon stripped from him. Recorded in Jer. 32 is the most elaborately described financial transaction in the Bible, a resounding statement of hope even within the context of Jeremiah's pessimistic message. This potter's field is the opposite of *Hakeldema*; it is a "field of hope" established against all reasonable expectations of deliverance. Jeremiah's "field at Anathoth" (v. 9) is a marker for unreasonable hope, a promise of redemption despite the impending Babylonian conquest. Jeremiah purchases this field like a child making a sandcastle in front of the rising tide. It is beautiful and senseless, hopeful in a manner that cannot be easily captivated by language.

Despite overwhelming odds that the "potter's field" purchase will be futile, Jeremiah buys the plot to emblematize hope. The kind of hope represented by this field is the radical sort that is not tied to predictable outcomes or easy resolutions. But the despair of Judas does not turn easily into happy returns. Those who wander *Hakeldema* are not comforted by platitudes. For Judas, everything is *not* going to "be all right." Any hope extended to Judas must be illogical, tuned to a frequency other than the darkness that closes in on all sides of the present reality. Jeremiah's hope is the hope of the future.

True responsibility reverses the loneliness of *Hakeldema*, standing in the chasm of despair that yawns on every side in a broken world. This is not a comfortable place to stand; folks like Judas have deep scars, anger, and resentment. Life is much more pleasant when standing far away from broken people. Furthermore, trying to address the world's tremendous overload of injustice can feel like throwing a Dixie Cup of water onto a raging fire. Christian hope offers a future to the despondent, without patronizingly manufacturing that hope out of human expectation. This is the kind of foolish hope that drives Jeremiah's purchase. Jeremiah *lives* the logic of a future reality that appears impossible given the logic of the present. What is stunning about Jeremiah's bold purchase of the "field at Anathoth" is the remarkable way it puts his ridiculous hope into tangible action (32:7-8). People are deserting their homes and towns and fleeing from the oncoming evil and devastation. Jeremiah buys a field.

Today, parallels to *Hakeldema* abound. Families ostracize the relative with an addiction or moral failing. Classmates leave the misfit to eat alone in the cafeteria. The middle class abandons the inner cities for safer suburbs. Even Christian denominations find themselves shifting their churches and operations away from the discomforts of urban life. Prisons are full of people caught in the lonely isolation of *Hakeldema*. Scores of elderly people find themselves sealed in by their walls, forgotten by most of society. Our nursing homes can sometimes look like *Hakeldema*. Foster children with physical, mental, and behavioral problems grow up moving restlessly between dozens of homes. All too often people wander the earth in lonely despair, suffering quietly and privately, never showing the world their internal anguish.

A community committed to justice, which Christians must surely be, belongs on the border of *Hakeldema*. Here bias and prejudice should be resisted, forgiveness should abound, and acts of foolish hope should be the norm. This cannot be a community obsessed with establishing or protecting its *own* identity. The wandering Judas seeks rest, comfort, healing, and forgiveness. We aren't just supposed to be Abel's keeper; he is friendly and gentle and unthreatening. We are to be keepers of Judas.

eight

SCAPEGOATS

A FRIEND OF MINE, who is ethnically Arab, was verbally and physically threatened in September 2001. An angry motorist, who accused him of carrying a bomb, called him "Osama." The experience was shocking for Kaseem, who had spent most of his life in a quiet and affluent Seattle suburb. Threatened with violence, Kaseem was told to "go back to your own country." The tension and discomfort experienced by Americans after the September 11 atrocities gave rise to a host of such instances all around the country. In the days following these horrific acts of terrorism, a shocking number of Americans with Arab, Persian, and Indian ethnicity were victims of threats, vandalism, and even murder. Seven people were killed in attacks attributed to retaliation for the violence of 9/11. In Somerset, Massachusetts, some teenagers tossed firebombs onto the roof of a convenience store, which was owned by an American citizen who was ethnically Indian. When he was apprehended, one teen said he "wanted to get back at the Arabs for what they did in New York."[1] Ironically, Sikhs often took the brunt of the abuse; unlike most Muslims, Sikh men usually wear turbans. Almost instantly, it became more difficult for people of Middle Eastern ethnicities to obtain jobs, passports, citizenship, and housing. A seemingly unprecedented amount of anger and anguish hung in the air. When human societies are destabilized, they cry out for blood. Understanding and addressing this impulse is a critical step on our journey to rethinking responsibility.

Among the more brilliant sociological and theological theories of the twentieth century was proposed by René Girard. Girard suggested that when social groups feel stressed, unstable, or threatened they tend to build up nervous energy.[2] Escalating tension increases the energy, making society an unstable pressure cooker. To address these social tensions, an "outlet" is needed. Humans, as we have seen, are highly capable of fighting back against adversity. But it is difficult to fight the forces that cause famine, drought, disease, and change. Unable to either fight or flee, human beings need a place to direct their reaction. People long to address the impulse to do *something* in the face of such frustrating social tension. With remarkable consistency across time and cultures, human communities have found release in directing pent-up energies and frustrations at a scapegoat. Girard traces this phenomenon through a wide variety of manifestations in human history. The "scapegoat mechanism" occurs with remarkable regularity across the religious traditions of the world, but he was surprised to find a unique manifestation of that theme in Judaism and Christianity.[3] His results may be extremely helpful as we ask what can be done about the great cloud of injustice that hangs over our societies.

As we have attempted to rethink responsibility, it has become clear that under close examination the concept of responsibility becomes overwhelming. How do we know which responsibility to address with the limited time, energy, and financial resources at our disposal? Who do we help first? Whose suffering, for which I find myself responsible, gets unaddressed? The larger answers to these questions will remain elusive. But since authentic responsibility can be paralyzing and overwhelming, it is vital that we seek a direction in which to begin this journey.

The scapegoat mechanism is based on the suspicion that violence acts as a release valve for social pressure. Something dark in human nature seems to surface when a group of people feels threatened. The Ku Klux Klan (KKK) provides a dramatic but obvious example of this, particularly in its earliest manifestations. The Klansmen, known for their white conical hats and robes, use terrorism and vigilante violence against ethnic and religious minorities. In reaction to social tensions and destabilization, KKK meetings sometimes included the ceremonial lynching of an African-American, a Jew, or a Roman Catholic.[4] These groups have traditionally been most active in the South and in small rural communities, in places where people recognize one another immediately. In small towns, faces and names are abundantly familiar. The Klan has therefore done most of its terrorizing at night. But even the cover of night is not sufficient to hide their faces from the world they terrorize. So they included masks in their costume to completely conceal their identities from their neighbors. The masks of the Klansmen are their ring of Gyges.

The Ku Klux Klan often becomes active in times of civil unrest, though it has also flourished as a social support system during times of relative rest. But when the economy is struggling, when war is immanent, when progressive politics is leading to uncomfortable change, the Klan has reacted violently. When society seems stable, when politics is stable, and the economy is flourishing, the Klan's activities fade. The KKK is an outlet that releases tension; in a frenzy of bloodthirsty violence, they turn the bodies of those who are "different" into their scapegoats. In his reflection on this violent mechanism, Girard points out that when a scapegoat is humiliated, ostracized, beaten, or killed, the rest of the community is united by their hatred of the victim. It matters little whether the lynched persons bear any actual guilt for the social woes. It is the lynching that matters; in one voice they cry out for blood, and together they take their frustrations out on a common target. The target is sometimes irrelevant to this ritual, which is really about unifying people who are isolated and terrified. Anxiety and stress lead people into a lonely *Hakeldema* of despair. As the mob gathers around the body of a scapegoat, the loneliness dissipates in shared hatred and violence.

Sometimes the reasoning used to select the scapegoat is absurd. In the famous witch hunts of colonial Salem, Massachusetts, nineteen men and women were hung on the basis of trivial and concocted evidence. Historians have noted that this was a tense time in Salem, with churches dividing and intense fear of the surrounding native nations.[5] The social strain of these factors, and many others, left the people vulnerable to atrocious scapegoating. It comes as no surprise that executions have traditionally been public spectacles. People unite behind the violence.

The concept of the scapegoat arises from Lev. 16, which describes a fascinating ritual of ancient animal sacrifice. The ritual merits a close look:

> When Aaron has finished making atonement . . . he shall bring forward the live goat. He is to lay both hands on the head of the live goat and confess over it all the wickedness and rebellion of the Israelites—all their sins—and put them on the goat's head. He shall send the goat away into the desert. . . . The goat will carry on itself all their sins to a solitary place *(vv. 20-22a, NIV).*

For the ancient Israelites there was a direct connection between their moral rectitude and the fate of their society. If they were practicing "wickedness and rebellion," they could expect drought, famine, and foreign invaders. Social turmoil and strife were considered a product of immorality, punishments from God. Israel considered its righteousness and sinfulness to be directly connected to the favor or wrath of God. For this reason, there is much at stake when it comes to the rituals designed to cleanse their nation of its impurities. The goat performs exactly this duty, receiving "all their sins" then carrying them far away from the community. The hapless goat wanders toward its certain death in the wilderness; the sins of the people disappear as wild animals devour the goat. The whole community receives ritual healing and forgiveness from the process. They are united both by the ritual and by their shared contribution to the death of the animal. Countless religious groups, ancient and modern, have been unified by the spectacle of animal or human sacrifice. They are united by the spectacle of creatures dying on holy altars, cast into fiery volcanoes, or devoured by wild beasts.

Though the ritual described in Leviticus is the source of the term "scapegoat," there are similar scapegoat rituals recorded in the writings of several Near Eastern cultures.[6] More often, inside and outside the Bible, it is *people* who play this role. One typical public ritual of execution was a stoning, a penalty broadly applied to wrongdoers from adulterers to Sabbath violators. Deuteronomy 21 infamously recommends stoning for rebellious children.[7] The execution of disobedient children is declared necessary because Israel must "purge the evil from your midst" (v. 21). This impulse is paralleled in many cultures and religious documents around the world.

No doubt they were reluctant to harm children, and it is likely that the "children" discussed in this passage are adolescent or adult children. This death sentence is driven by a need to keep the land *pure*, and when people execute violators that defile the land, they protect society.

When ancient Israel executed by stoning, the whole community lined up to throw a rock at the violator until he or she was pummeled or buried to death. The process is an organized form of mob violence, in which each hurler has the cleansing and unifying role of tossing a single stone. No single rock kills the victim; it is all the rocks together that enact the execution. The story told in John 8, concerning Jesus and the woman caught in adultery, takes on new meaning in light of the scapegoat mechanism. When Jesus says, "If any one of you is without sin, let him be the first to throw a stone at her" (v. 7, NIV), the angry mob disperses when their mechanistic turn to violence is exposed.

Girard uses this biblical concept to interpret the religious and social forces that lead to mob violence and scapegoating across history. In the fourteenth century, when the Black Plague was decimating Europe's population, destabilized Christians often looked for a source of this phantom killer. Jews became a logical and vulnerable target. Accusing Jews of poisoning wells or spreading the disease, mobs would round up Jewish people and execute them publicly. The destabilized community found stability in their common, anti-Semitic violence. It mattered little that Jews were as likely to die from the plague as anyone else. Girard brilliantly draws examples from ancient Greek mythology to the twentieth century. His thesis is compelling. When people feel cold panic settle into their bones, they find strange comfort in abusing the bodies of defenseless scapegoats. These can be very *good people*, religious people with no obvious intention to do harm to others. And yet the damage can be shocking. As Steven Weinberg wrote, "With or without religion, you would have good people doing good things and evil people doing evil things. But for good people to do evil things, that takes religion."[8]

The story of Judas, which has been helpful in exploring the concepts of community and responsibility, also classically follows Girard's thesis. Judas is treated dispassionately in Mark and compassionately in Matthew. But in Luke and John, the later gospels, Judas becomes increasingly demonized. Christian history after the close of the New Testament has been no friendlier to Judas. His story and treachery have become synonymous with pure evil. Judas has become a human being that Christians are excused for loathing. For this human, at any rate, hatred is appropriate. The sympathy felt by Matthew for Judas's remorse and repentance is retained in a single verse (see 27:3); otherwise Judas has been a perfect scapegoat. For centuries Christians have found release for their anxiety at Christ's suffering through common hatred of Judas. In early and medieval Christian art, Judas is frequently depicted as only half-human. Dante reserves his deepest recesses of hell for Judas, who "has the greatest punishment."[9]

The manslayer also runs from this scapegoat mechanism, which seeks to cure pain by inflicting suffering on others. The irate blood avenger pursues the manslayer, "hot" with anger. What drives the blood avenger to overturn every stone to find the person who killed his kin? The impulse to punish and extract blood from *someone*, regardless of guilt or intention, is Girard's scapegoat mechanism. The wisdom of Girard's theory is evident in the overwhelming repetition of this pattern.

When communities are most deeply frightened or threatened, the scapegoat mechanism can lead to mass hysteria, where societies look for blood without discretion. Like an addict feels the increasing need for a fix, desperate times drive societies to seek stability through violence. It is the deepest and saddest of ironies when Christians perform these acts of scapegoating. In its first centuries, the members of the struggling religious group called Christians were routinely martyred to satisfy the need for scapegoat-violence amid an instable Roman Empire.

Scapegoat-violence only alleviates tension for a while, providing cathartic release for the pressures of society. When anxiety rebuilds, the need for violence builds along with it. Scapegoat-violence is the drug of choice used to treat human social tension. Like all addictive drugs, this "rush" meets a need only to ask for more. Psychologists and neuroscientists often point out that the rush that comes from violent behavior performs similar brain functions as narcotics. The modern world is strung out on this brand of violence. We watched as 9/11 left the United States looking for blood. Sang Toby Keith, in a song he called "Courtesy of the Red, White, and Blue (The Angry American)": "Soon as we could see clearly through our big black eye, / Man we lit up your world like the fourth of July."[10] Violence begets violence. There are many results of the anti-Muslim sentiment that swept the United States in the years that have followed, including reckless foreign conflict, discrimination, racial profiling, and ethnic violence. At its core, wounded America is subconsciously looking for a violent "fix" to address a violent problem.

In the scapegoat mechanism we have more than just another overwhelming level of responsibility to address. The flip side of this frightening impulse in human society is that we now catch a glimpse of the direction in which responsibility must be focused. By identifying this force we also find wisdom to address a pattern that has long cried out for correction. In *refusing to scapegoat* we can begin to move past the cycles of violence that reinforce and redouble social injustice. And it is in Christianity's unique relationship to scapegoat-violence that Girard finds potential release from this abysmal repetition of violence and vengeance.

Girard points out that Christianity is unique among all the world's religions for its peculiar and unusual relationship to the scapegoat. In many cultures, the scapegoat—whether human or animal—must die to appease the smoldering anger of a vexed deity. But in the Christian gospel, it is Jesus Christ who becomes the scapegoat. This, claims Girard, is radically unique and sets Christianity apart from the countless pagan forms of scapegoat-violence. In Christianity, God endures and therefore shames the scapegoat mechanism. God absorbs the violence of the world, rather than redoubling it. Refusing vengeance, or even retaliation, Jesus moves "like a lamb to the slaughter" (Isa. 53:7, NIV). The rhythmic repetition of violence is shattered. The ongoing need for victimization and suffering is interrupted by the shocking *worship* of the scapegoat.

The implications for Christian communities are profound. The scapegoat is *Christ*. This means that the person whom society is strongly inclined to victimize is the one whose welfare must be most carefully safeguarded. Girard's theological analysis is consistent with some of Jesus' most memorable parables and teachings. "Love your enemy," says Jesus, "and pray for those who persecute you" (Matt. 5:44, NIV). The Good Samaritan resists the powerful urge to scapegoat the "ethnic" other (see Luke 10). In Matt. 25, Jesus claims that whatever has been done to those who are hungry, thirsty, naked, sick, and imprisoned has been done *to him*. In this powerful parable Jesus places *himself* in the place of the people who are easiest to scapegoat in society. To scapegoat, even in the seemingly legitimate manner of shunning prisoners, is an offense to the "Son of man" himself.

So here we begin to see some light on this uncertain path toward authentic responsibility. To be responsible is to refuse to scapegoat. But the injunction goes beyond *avoiding* the impulse to single someone out for "therapeutic" violence. Responsibility *protects* the scapegoat; it stands between the scapegoat and the violent mob. For Christians it is abundantly obvious—to scapegoat is to join the throng that cried out for Jesus' death. Christianity starkly and resoundingly opposes the impulse to scapegoat. Christianity resists the pervasive impulse to blood-let for the sake of righting the injustice of the world.

Perhaps we can learn an even more vital lesson from Girard's theory and the pervasive evidence of scapegoating across modern and ancient history. A pressing problem has been building across our investigations into human responsibility. The most difficult question, when it comes to responsibility, is clearly *who* warrants our limited time and attention. This question may be partly answered by the scapegoat theory and its implications for daily life. We are responsible for more than we know and more than we can outline or anticipate. But Christian responsibility turns its primary attention to the scapegoats, to the poor, to the fleeing manslayer, to the widow, to the hungry, and to the orphan. This will not serve as a full or final answer to our questions about responsibility, but it is a considerable start. To the question, "Who should I help first?" the answer must be *the victim*. Society has many victims, more than we can count or help. But it is here, in the faces of those society calls "least," that we find the first movement of responsibility. And given the overwhelming nature of responsibility, it is good to have a place to start.

Concern for "the least of these" often looks both foolish and dangerous. Caring for victims means absorbing pain and anger that are easily and more comfortably avoided. But leaning in this direction does not mean reinventing the wheel. Concern for victims runs deep in Christian and Jewish scripture. Fields are left ungleaned for the poor, widows, orphans, and aliens. Whole cities are to be built just to accommodate the possible innocence of an accused murderer. Samaritans stop to help a dangerous foreigner in the ditch. Christ is found in the cup of cold water handed to the person dying of thirst. The rich young ruler's morality is incomplete until it is turned to the poor. To utter the word "God" in Christianity is already to invoke the face of the victim, the social outcast, the scapegoat.

How might this look? History, fortunately, provides us with a number of answers. In the Middle Ages, mobs riled up by racial and religious tensions would sweep through European towns. In the name of the Crusades, of which most of them were not a part, these people would ransack towns looking for Jews and Muslims to slaughter. European life was not particularly pleasant during medieval times, leading to plenty of suffering and anger. The "Christian" marauders, clearly looking for a scapegoat to sacrifice, were dangerous and threatening. What is interesting about this dark chapter in Christian history is that some Christians refused to bend to the will of the ethnic and religious hysteria. Priests and faithful Christians took the risk of hiding Muslims and Jews in their homes and churches. In the midst of one of Christianity's ugliest chapters, we find remarkable hospitality and responsibility. Faithful Christians crafted a "city of refuge" for the frightened and fleeing Muslim, purchasing a place of peace at the risk of their own lives. They refused to join in the frenzied violence of scapegoating.

This heroic ability to stand bravely against violent impulses is repeated during World War II, as *some* Christians hid and protected Jews from Hitler's atrocious attempt at complete genocide. Steven Spielberg made famous a man named Oskar Schindler, who risked his life as a comfortable Nazi businessman to save dozens of Jewish lives. These are concrete, if dramatic, examples of people refusing to participate in scapegoat-violence and struggling to give life to people caught on the wrong side of the hordes that cry out for violence. The scapegoat mechanism is primarily about exclusion for the sake of social cohesion, which is precisely the role given to Jews by Adolf Hitler's Nazi Party. They were radically excluded in a massive instance of scapegoat-violence, and the energy and social cohesion produced by this genocide fueled the meteoric rise of the Third Reich. But scapegoating must also be resisted in its quieter and less dramatic forms. People are excluded and shunned by social groups around the world, suffering a subtler form of this same impulse. One does not need nooses or gas chambers to scapegoat.

Brave Harriet Tubman, a former slave, risked her life on thirteen missions into the American South to free other slaves. When the United States was locking people away in droves during the Red Scare of the 1950s, *some* Christians refused to participate in the witch hunt. After the fall of apartheid in South Africa, decades of gruesome injustice hung over an entire nation. In the face of an overwhelming impulse to retaliate against former oppressors, South African leaders Nelson Mandela and Archbishop Desmond Tutu insisted on an intense program to prevent retaliatory violence. The Truth and Reconciliation Commission struggled to name and identify injustices in order to forgive and reconcile. In remarkable and gritty fashion, the commission identified and forgave a long list of grievances. They walked the tightwire between overlooking injustice and longing to see the pendulum of racial violence come to a stop. The Truth and Reconciliation Commission, which some other countries have tried in vain to imitate, is a beautiful example of unraveling the scapegoat impulse.

Ironically, the sinister forces of scapegoat-violence also give rise to a profound compass that may guide us beyond the indecision that arises from competing responsibilities. Lost in the sea of unlimited responsibility, how does one authentically do *anything*? An answer to this question will be elusive, but we can find some orientation by looking to the person or groups around us who suffer under the social impulse to resolve tension by bloodletting. If one wonders where to begin to act responsibly, the scapegoat is a good place to start. To paraphrase Jesus' words in Matt. 25: "Whatever you have done to the scapegoat, you have done to me."

To be Christian is to stand between the mob and the goat.

nine

RENT

IN *THE BRAVE ONE* (2007) Jodi Foster plays Erica Bain, a radio host who walks around New York City and broadcasts her experiences from the sights and sounds of the streets. Bain is brutally attacked beneath an overpass while walking through the Strangers' Gate entrance to Central Park with her fiancé, who dies from the injuries. Bain is left to cope with the brokenness of her body and the loss of her beloved. Her slow physical recovery eventually enables her to leave the hospital and return home to an apartment full of memories. She bears the physical and psychological scars of trauma: her memories of the attack are blurred, her body shakes and jumps on the streets she once walked with confidence, and she begins to see profound danger in the strangers who walk beside her.

Bain is caught in a tremendous tension; she has made a living from translating her experiences on the street into radio broadcasts. Her work has made the enormous city of New York smaller, more intimate, less chaotic, and more respectable. Now she feels nothing of the city's charm and sees only danger and animosity in the faces around her. The panic that overwhelms Bain drives her into a gun shop, where she learns she must wait thirty days to get a permit. Convinced she wouldn't survive a month without the protection of a firearm, she buys one illegally. But the trauma of her attack and her frustration at the inability of law enforcement to find her fiancé's killers lead Bain down a dark path of vigilante violence. Her walks lead her into the dark corners of New York, where she kills thugs and pimps and criminals. Bain shocks herself at the new person she has become. Her hands, which shook violently when she first fired her gun, become steady and sure. Her first killings are potentially justifiable as self-defense, but then she hunts down a high-profile businessman who has narrowly escaped prosecution for child abuse.

The film's strongest point is certainly the acting of Foster, who portrays a woman *rent* (ripped away) from her former self and transformed by trauma into someone completely different. Her transformation horrifies her; she realizes that the attack at Strangers' Gate has given rise to a stranger that lurks within her. Her former life is in shambles, but not the sort of pieces that can be put back together again. Nietzsche famously wrote, and singer Kanye West more recently rapped, "That which does not kill me makes me stronger."[1] For all his sufferings, Nietzsche must not have been thinking of this sort of trauma. For that matter, anyone who has been permanently shattered knows that Nietzsche was dead wrong.

In this chapter we turn our attention to the problem of human brokenness and the way that abuse, trauma, and sorrow influence responsibility. People find their lives damaged, broken and incomplete in an infinite number of ways. Any simple summary of human suffering and anxiety invariably fails to take this diversity seriously. For our purposes here we will talk about two different types of brokenness. This chapter is titled "Rent" because it seeks to address the way human lives are ripped by violence and trauma. The word "rent" carries with it passive connotations; we are *rent* by circumstance and events outside of our control. Bain is *rent* by her beating and the loss of her fiancé; she plays no active role in the complete upheaval of her life.

I have reserved the term "torn" for the next chapter and confined the meaning of "torn" to refer to the times when we are pulled between competing responsibilities. The division is somewhat artificial, since these two fields of brokenness have tremendous overlap. Consider the plight of Peter, who is *rent* by the death of Jesus but *torn* by his own betrayal. The complexity of lived experiences makes it difficult to disentangle the various ways that we suffer brokenness. For this reason these two chapters are thoroughly intertwined. But the passive experience of violence and trauma present a unique and tender problem for our study of responsibility. I am naming that the experience of being *rent*.

Abuse, trauma, brokenness, and suffering have an undeniable, tangible, and direct influence on responsibility. People who are broken are cast, forcibly, into a defensive and self-protective posture. This retreat is abundantly healthy and appropriate. But what can be said about the question of responsibility for those who have been rent? How might we speak of extreme hospitality in light of those who have been traumatized? My claim throughout this book has been that we are *more* responsible than we realize. These words fall heavy on the ears of a person who has been subjected to someone else's profound irresponsibility. It is unhealthy and unwise to wrench oneself out of the despondency of suffering and directly into self-renouncing hospitality. Bain's character illustrates this well; she returns to the streets long before she is capable of walking them in a safe or healthy fashion.

The situation is tender. Are people in the darkness of this suffering to consider themselves stripped of the very capacity to be responsible? Throughout this book I have argued that responsibility is the very centerpiece of humanity; quite literally, I *am* my responsibility. Does this rob the wounded of their very humanity? These questions are as important as anything we can investigate in a book about reconsidering responsibility.

We must take seriously the process of mourning, adjustment, and healing that yawns in front of the sufferer. By no fault of his or her own, the traumatized is banished into a tremendously difficult journey. Deep trauma leaves a person far from the edgy place of extreme responsibility. The plight of the *rent*, which has driven so many of our reflections in this book, now takes center stage. It is one thing to struggle to prevent offensive violence. But what sort of responsibility can be pushed onto people who have been rent? In order to address this question we must look even more closely at the dynamics of human relationships. The discussion of responsibility typically focuses on the flashiness of actions and behaviors. But responsibility begins before activity, in a choice that may seem simple before we have been rent. To be responsible, we must first be able to respond.

The band Bright Eyes, in their song "Waste of Paint," sing a verse about a woman whose husband has betrayed her. She first tries to convince herself she is "grateful for all that happened." But then she weeps, admitting she has been rent from her former self by the unfaithfulness of her husband. She retreats from the world in which she once flourished, swearing to "never clean another mess, or fold his shirts, or look her best. *She [is] free to waste away, alone.*"[2] Suffering does indeed drive us away from others; we cannot blame the wounded for recoiling from human contact, let alone tremendous responsibility. In seclusion, and in despondency, there is a certain freedom that was denied during the moments of trauma. The moment of offense is far from free; the perpetrator, human or otherwise, traps the other person. Despondency can therefore be a kind of liberation, a freedom from the oppressive and painful outside. Better to be "free to waste away, alone" than to be trapped in the abusive world of the other. This kind of brokenness often drives people back from the relational edge in which *active* responsibility lives. And the blame for this tension simply cannot be laid at the feet of the wounded.

Many people find themselves barely capable of getting out of bed; how can they be expected to take on more than their share of responsibility? Perhaps the term "despondency" describes this state well. Interestingly, this word shares a common Latin root with the term "responsibility": *spond/spons* has the root meaning of "covenant" or "pledge." The person who is despondent is outside of the covenantal relationship with other persons. To be despondent, for any reason, is to be positioned far away from the dangerous place of mutual trust. And this distance is absolutely mandatory for any movement toward healing.

But it cannot be forgotten that despondency and responsibility are logically contradictory. For our purposes here I will push the term "despondency" beyond its typical usage. More than blank stares and distant emotions, I take "despondency" to indicate any wounded retreat from meaningful relationships. For our purposes here, despondency is what happens when we have been traumatized and therefore barricade ourselves emotionally from the world that has caused us pain. In *The Brave One*, Bain certainly seems to be active, but she remains emotionally despondent, unable to feel the weight of her own violent actions.

Defined in this way, the state of despondency is a kind of defense mechanism. Despondency is not evil or sinful; it is a kind of fight for life, an act of resistance against both pain and death. People who have been rent and who consequently find themselves despondent are faced with innumerable obstacles. There is no way to do justice to the diversity of suffering and despondency that abounds in our broken world. We can also be certain that no uniform response will be appropriate given the variety of degrees and manners in which people are wounded.

Undeniably, trauma, abuse, and disaster can hinder and even disable our ability to respond to others. This barrier presents a potentially disastrous problem for our discussions of responsibility. It is simply unacceptable to insinuate that people who have been broken are by definition *irresponsible*, because their abusers have driven them to despondency. Despondency is *not* the same thing as irresponsibility, and the importance of this distinction is as vital as anything written in this book. To be broken by others is to be rent from one's own capacity to respond, to be divulged of the very mechanisms through which we pursue the healthy communities that make and sustain our humanity. Many sufferers of traumatic abuse report that this consequence is as damaging as the abuse itself. In the faces of others we find life and meaning, but when we are rent, we instinctively retreat from these sources of life. Pain turns us inward.

We walk on perilously thin ice when we talk about the relationship between trauma and responsibility. In this sense, the plight of the wounded calls for us to make a massive disclaimer about the forceful calls to responsibility articulated throughout this book. The danger is that the imperative to be responsible can be turned into a tool of manipulation to force a traumatized person into action, sometimes redoubling the suffering. Responsibility is not first of all activity but a prior connection to others. The fact that being responsible typically takes a very active form blinds us to the more important foundation of all responsible activity.

To understand how suffering and vulnerability relate to responsibility we must gingerly address the long and *sacred* road between despondency and responsibility. The movement out of despondency travels first to the place where a person is *responsive*. And every person retains the right to be unresponsive in the face of such pain. The movement toward healing must be chosen, not imposed. The choice to be responsive, rather than despondent, is not necessarily a stepping-stone to some more important or active form of responsibility. When a widow chooses to mourn in community instead of in solitude, this choice need not be driven by any particular goal. Responsiveness need not lead anywhere; it can be as beautiful and simple as an embrace or a squeezed hand. The act of response, even if it occurs in one's final breath, binds one human life to another. We should say very little about what people can or should do when faced with this kind of brokenness.

For those who have been rent, the road forward moves first into relationships of healthy interdependence. Despondency leads us away from community, wandering the lonely *Hakeldema* of despair. The choice to be in community is a difficult and perilous one for people who have been burned by others. This move into a mode of responsiveness is gritty and frightening. But for those who have been rent, responsiveness is the alternative to lonely isolation. The despondent are in need of safe haven, of a community of healing. This is the very community that failed to materialize for Erica Bain in *The Brave One*. Left to heal herself, her despondency turned to defensiveness and eventually violence. Her movement away from despondency began when a single friend told her, "There's plenty of ways to die, but you have to figure out a way to live."

This kind of loss-of-wholeness is not foreign to the Christian story. All four Gospels speak of the Galilean women who watch nearby as Jesus is crucified.[3] Their presence at the cross stands in intentional contrast to the scattered disciples, who remain inactive throughout the crucifixion and burial of Jesus. When Matthew pauses to tell us about the women who watch Jesus die, he seems to do so in passing, as though filling time between the important moments of action in the narrative. Storytellers rarely take time to note witnesses who do not tangibly influence the narrative. Matthew's reference to people watching "from a distance" or "sitting" at a gravesite appears unnecessary and tangential (27:55, 61, NIV), at least to the modern reader. This narrative has important events to unfold; the women who watch from a distance and follow Jesus' body to the tomb appear to do nothing to push the story along. Even some commentators consider Matthew's brief discussion of these women parenthetical. They are, after all, only "looking on from a distance" (v. 55).[4]

The watchfulness and patience of the women may not register as significant to all commentators, but it serves a most remarkable function in all four gospels. The structure of this story situates these women as all that is left of the movement surrounding Jesus. They are the only tangible link between the dynamic movement and flurry of activity that precedes the crucifixion and the darkness that follows. This group of women, Mary Magdalene and Mother Mary in particular, are the last at the cross, the last to linger at the tomb, and the first at the tomb on Sunday morning. The male disciples disappear from the narrative after they scatter in the garden and Peter denies Jesus in the courtyard. Judas wanders to his lonely suicide.

Movements and charismatic leaders come and go, and their followings dissipate in the rather predictable fashion described of Jesus' disciples. Friends flee; loyal followers wonder how far to take their allegiance. Most of Jesus' followers scatter and disappear from the story at Gethsemane. Peter follows Jesus long enough to deny him vehemently and ends up weeping "bitterly" (Matt. 26:75). None of the Twelve risks his life to protect Jesus' body from the ignominy of being cast with Judas into a field to decay. This task falls to Joseph of Arimathea, who joins the women in their faithfulness to the corpse of Jesus.

These women are the remainder of Jesus' band. Like anyone who sees a loved one die, or a dream completely shattered, they are *rent*. The male disciples, too, are rent by the events of Good Friday. But the male and female followers of Jesus respond to his death in breathtakingly different ways.

The disciples, including Judas, wander into a Saturday of lonely despondency. The women, as deeply broken, cling together in mourning outside the tomb of Jesus. As Matthew winds down his Good Friday story, he describes the hospitality of Joseph, who buries Jesus and then heads home. In a stirring depiction of responsive mourning, Matthew tells us that "Mary Magdalene and the other Mary were there, sitting opposite the tomb" (27:61). Mary and Mary are broken; they have experienced deep and wrenching loss.

This is a quiet moment, lost in the earthshaking events that come before and afterward in the gospel narratives. The earth stays still as Joseph wraps (and probably washes) the body, and the rocks beneath the feet of Mary and Mary do not split as they sit opposite the tomb. The women who persist quietly beside cross and tomb have consistently supported Jesus' life and ministry; they have birthed, nurtured, raised, fed, clothed, and supported Jesus. The disciples have come and gone. These women remain. And in their patience and communal mourning we find tremendous wisdom for the times when we, too, are *rent*.

Is it coincidental that these are *women* who remain faithful even in their brokenness? These women have loved Jesus in the gritty, nurturing fashion sometimes less familiar to males. Their support of Jesus is not merely intellectual or spiritual: it is embodied. Jesus' mother offered her womb to nurture him into life, and she continued to "womb" Jesus even in his death. The flashy parts of the passion story belong to the men, but at the margins of this story we find a feminine response to trauma that is clearly lost on most of the men in this story. It was Mary and Mary who did not turn away from one another in despondency.

Perhaps it is deeply important that in their brokenness these women do not *do* anything noteworthy, at least nothing that Matthew describes. It seems sufficient to devote this single verse of Scripture to their posture and position relative to Jesus: they sit together opposite the tomb. Mark emphasizes what they witnessed, providing the equally uneventful note that they "saw where the body was laid" (15:47). In the face of brokenness we long to get to work fixing a problem, to fight or flee, to busy ourselves in some direction. But there is a painful irony that arises when we are rent; our impulse to be active works against us. The drive to act must be suspended here in the moments of Holy Saturday. Before one can turn to responsible action, one must chose to be *responsive*. One must mourn in community, turning away from the despondent and lonely night endured by Peter and Judas. Something deeper is at work here, deeper even than the actions of responsibility. The very basis of responsibility is the dwelling of humans face-to-face. Mary Magdalene and Mary the mother of Jesus *face* one another. In a quiet but stunningly important move, they allow their brokenness to drive them back to the very roots of all responsibility: the face of the other.

It may sound ironic to suggest that responsibility calls for inactivity, sitting, waiting, and mourning. But the new life that may come on the other side of brokenness will seldom be recognizable to people who frantically struggle to put pieces back together. Even after the Easter narratives, Mary and Mary do not get Jesus back in the way they had him before Good Friday. They mourn the loss of their friend and son, and in doing so they must let him go. As Jesus says to Mary Magdalene in the garden, perhaps painfully, "Do not cling to Me" (John 20:17, NKJV). People who have been rent have a number of reasons to "cling" to the life taken from them. But moving into the unforeseen future of new life requires a release—a letting go—that we can seldom perform alone. This stage of mourning and adjustment may require a space for healing, a reprieve from the pressures of extreme moral obligation. Only communities can grant this kind of reprieve, both by insulating the wounded and by fulfilling her obligations as she heals.

Bain is a fictional character, but Foster plays her well, showing the anxiety of a person traumatized. She is wrenched and broken in a permanent manner. In far less obvious and dramatic ways, many people are routinely rent from possibilities they may never be able to actualize. It is the dream of wholeness that presents enormous obstacles to any movement out of despondency.

What we see in bright and glaring lines on the silver screen appears in less obvious ways in everyday life. We teach our children to dream big, to shoot for the moon, and to disregard people who might instruct them otherwise. And well we should. But perhaps our children are poorly equipped to deal with the experiences of grief, anxiety, and brokenness that life too often delivers. In big and small ways, we are routinely rent. We are ripped away from people we love, injured by the carelessness of others, wounded by the malice of our enemies, and even punished by the cruelty of people long dead. We are rent by accidental damages, natural disasters, and fires nobody meant to light.

We do not deal well with this heartbreaking aspect of our lives. When humans experience brokenness, we are inclined to denial or depression, and sometimes both. These inclinations are often natural and understandable; who could expect a widower or a widow to take this loss in stride? In the face of brokenness, a "mythology of wholeness" teaches us to dream of getting all the pieces put back together. But when people experience real loss, or are broken in a way that cannot be mended, this myth can wreak havoc on every aspect of human life.

Children of divorce provide an obvious example. For many children, the separation of parents leads to an array of emotional responses. Among the most common reactions to divorce is an unhealthy fantasy that a child's parents will reunite. The hope isn't entirely unfounded, since some people do remarry the very people they have divorced. But no child psychologist would recommend fostering this hope in a child. For children rent by divorce, the only healthy route leads through a process of mourning and acceptance. Children, for the most part, experience the divorce of their parents in passivity, playing no active role in the breakup of their families.

In 1993 Robin Williams starred in the comedy *Mrs. Doubtfire*, playing a divorcé who masquerades as a female nanny to be closer to his children. According to Williams, the writers originally intended to depict a reunification of the divorced couple at the end of the film. Williams and costar Sally Field resisted the plotline out of fear that such a story line might inspire unhealthy hope among children that their divorced parents would reunite.[5] The dream of wholeness, of the restoration of a past that is gone forever, is a natural reaction to divorce and brokenness. But this dream is a detour, not a route toward healing.

One of the most wrenching and difficult aspects of being rent is coming to the admission that we cannot always make a full recovery from the damages done to us. It isn't just physical traumas, like Bain's attack, that leave us permanently changed. For the sufferer of wrenching trauma, physical or otherwise, there is no road forward that completely obliterates the brokenness of a person's past. The reality is profoundly unfair: Why should a rapist be allowed to rewire the mental and emotional lives of the people he has already physically mistreated? Why is it that abusers continue to torment long after they are dead? As if the abuse itself were not bad enough, the recipients are left to cope with a life permanently altered. The word "unfair" does not begin to describe this common scenario.

It is true, of course, that people sometimes make remarkable and seemingly impossible recoveries from brokenness. But we have to admit these are exceptions to a cruel rule of life. Most of the time, when we are rent, some aspect of the damage is permanent. This does not make the Cinderella story of full recovery any less appealing or tempting. We long for harsh realities of the past to be obliterated from our histories; and there is nothing wrong with this longing. But if untended and unaddressed, this desire can leave us despondent, wandering the streets of life in search of a missing piece that can never be found. And as we wander, we move further and further from responsibility, often distancing ourselves from the very faces that might lead us toward healing and life.

There are many ways to avoid confronting our brokenness. We can distract ourselves with an endless stream of new stimuli. Through substance abuse we can literally self-medicate ourselves into numbness. It is no coincidence that the abuse of painkillers is a skyrocketing form of drug abuse.[6] When we are rent, we long to kill the pain. And here we find the spiral of despondency. We are not mended by our retreats into the numbing worlds of eating disorders, cutting, drug abuse, and self-loathing. One moment of despondency leads to another. The movement out of the covenantal realm of human relationships can become addictive. Many people who have been wounded report that it is only in this enclosed world of self-abuse that they find any measure of control when they feel utterly helpless. They are free to waste away, alone.

People who have been emotionally and physical rent are obviously not whole according to the mythology of wholeness. This myth is preserved and repeated in the "happily ever after" motif of fairy tales and Disney movies. According to this common myth, there must always be a route forward that restores and reverses the damage. But we are so locked into a cultural mythology of wholeness that we instinctively think of people who do not meet the criterion of wholeness as somehow defective or even less than fully human. The struggle to put together the broken pieces can torment and consume. Perhaps the first step away from emotional despondency is to release the fantasy that the damages can be completely undone.

We must also remain mindful that *no one is whole*. Not everyone is broken in the same way. The mythology of wholeness can trap us in endless cycles of self-deception, despondency, self-loathing, disappointment, and despair. The path to life leads through facing others, being responsive, adjusting to the life that remains in the wake of trauma, and learning to live as people who have been wounded.

Much more could be said about this, and one small chapter can only attempt to say with broad strokes what needs to be explored in much greater detail. I will leave it to other authors to explore the different ways that "facing" can lead the wounded toward healing, adjustment, and new life. The movement away from despondency may involve a counselor, a therapist, good friends, a church community, and a host of other safe "faces" with whom the wounded can relearn to respond. For now, we must defend an exception to the rule of extreme hospitality; we are to be responsible even for the despondency of the wounded. For the sake of people who are rent, Christians must craft communities of *refuge*.

The first step is to sit face-to-face with others, as ironic as that advice may sound given the imperative to act that has driven most of this text. All acts of responsibility have their origin in the fundamental face-to-face relation between human beings. When we are rent, by no fault of our own, the faces of others can become distant and strange and irrelevant. The movement toward life is a movement through the face of the other and a movement against the despondent retreat into oneself. For the broken, this is no easy step; it is often the faces of others who have caused the suffering. Yet it is the face-to-face relationships with others that give rise to healing and new life. In the difficult turn from despondency the wounded person makes the gritty choice to do more than just survive trauma. For people lost in the aimless *Hakeldema* of suffering, the wisdom of Mary and Mary provides a direction in which to move. Their movement toward each other is a movement away from the loneliness of despondency; this is a form of mourning that leads to life. When they chose to weep together, with the stone of Jesus' tomb between them, they chose life.

ten

TORN

IDEALISM runs thick through the veins of many college students, and I was no exception. The clarion calls for dangerous hospitality that appear in Christian Scripture inspired me to think there should be no exceptions to hospitality. A sermon on the parable of the Good Samaritan left me scanning roadsides and ditches, looking for a "stranger" to whom I could be neighbor. It wasn't long before I was regularly picking up hitchhikers. I struggled to destroy any filter by which I might pick up one person and leave the other fading in my rearview mirror. This led to some scary moments, to be sure. Driving alone across the empty plains of eastern Oregon State, I saw two large men beside the road with their thumbs in the air. Alone in the car, I was reluctant to pick up multiple hitchhikers. I gulped and pulled to the side of the road, convincing myself that this was exactly the sort of risk taken by Jesus' Good Samaritan.

The men were impressed that I stopped; they weren't expecting anyone but a trucker to pick them up in the middle of nowhere. They rode two hundred miles with me that day, and as they climbed out of my car, I felt confident that I had done the Good Samaritan one better. I had stopped and helped *two* dangerous strangers on the roadside. My fiancé was not pleased with my tale when I proudly described my high moral ground. She wondered, justifiably, if I had considered the risk to *her* when I pulled to the side of the road. I didn't bother telling my parents, who would have been even more perturbed. I continued to pick up hitchhikers for many years until a major event curtailed my somewhat self-righteous hospitality—kids.

Now when I drive down the road, I regularly have six brown eyes staring at me from the backseat. They are vulnerable, almost defenseless without my protection. As I roll down the roads of life, a certain internal battle occurs every time I pass someone trying to bum a ride alongside the road. I've seen the movies and read the news stories of hitchhiking gone awry. My impulse to be hospitable to the stranger on the side of the road comes into direct conflict with the responsibility to be a good father. I feel both responsibilities to the core of my being. I am *torn*, but the big brown eyes always win.

There are exceptions, of course. I play a painful game of risk management. I may stop to help *some* people with the kids in the car, if I find the strangers unthreatening. Perhaps I might lend my cell phone to someone with a broken-down vehicle. But there is no doubt that I would drive past those same two men I picked up along a lonely highway in Oregon. There might be plenty of seats in our minivan, but if my kids are sitting behind me, I am noticeably less likely to stop. Clearly there is no shame in preserving one's children. But the impulse to protect one's own is certainly corruptible; gated communities in sterilized suburbia are constructed to be far away from the dangers of the unpleasantness of the world's suffering. So it may not be the case that I make an immoral or irresponsible choice as I watch the needy stranger fade in my rearview mirror. But I am undoubtedly torn between responsibilities. I drive past and leave behind the manslayer, the scapegoat, the Judas, the victim. That I make reasonable choices in the midst of this particular situation is only part of the struggle. What we are up against, in an infinite number of ways every day, is *competing responsibilities*. This is the problem of justice; morality can proclaim it good to play the Samaritan and care for the stranger. But the question of justice asks how one can live in a world with so many people in the ditch.

We do not get to live as long as we'd like. We make hard choices between potential careers, spouses, and friendships. Some of our decisions are bad, and some are good. Most are somewhere in between, and we feel the bittersweetness of life. This chapter deals with a somewhat milder tension than the issues discussed in the previous chapter. Even when we are not *rent* by crushing events that leave our lives in shambles, we still find ourselves repeatedly *torn*. We are often torn between two very good roads through life. To paraphrase Thomas Aquinas: "Every choice is a renunciation."[1] To be human is to be torn.

More than one Christian has been troubled by the shocking declaration by Jesus in Luke 14: "Whoever comes to me and does not hate father and mother, wife and children, brothers and sisters, yes, and even life itself, cannot be my disciple" (v. 26). When Jesus told his disciples they must "hate" their families to follow him, he could not have been advocating any kind of malicious sentiment toward loved ones. Jesus knew that life is torn and that following him would lead to a tearing and a choosing. The pathways of life, no matter how closely they follow religious or moral guidelines, will inevitably leave us torn.

And perhaps here it should be noted that people who are *rent* and people who are *torn* share an essential form of incompletion. There are infinitely diverse ways of being incomplete. But the myth of "wholeness" that torments victims is not entirely dissimilar from the myth of "completely fulfilled responsibility" that irks me when I pass a wandering hitchhiker. When we are honest, we come to realize that despite our diversity, we all lack wholeness and completion.

The way we deal with life's incompleteness has a profound influence on responsibility. The dream of completeness and wholeness has its roots in a very healthy impulse, a drive for the fullness of life that is beautiful and richly human. It is difficult to live in the tensions of an incomplete life, to settle for anything less than complete fulfillment. Perhaps a few lucky people avoid major calamity in life, but in most cases we find ourselves pretending that we are untorn, whole, or at least that the dream of completeness has not died. But engaging the realm of justice and responsibility requires a forfeiture of this fantasy. If we are responsible at the elevated level described in this book, then we are not and can never be whole until all people are whole. We live in a world full of people torn and rent, and the call of responsibility binds us to one another in a common aching for healing and completion. It is for the sake of this world, for the hitchhiker and the victim, that we must suspend our obsession with personal wholeness and completion.

Here we find that a mythology of individualized self-fulfillment stands squarely in our way if we mean to place responsibility at the center of Christianity and Christian community. This myth venerates the able-bodied, virile, hypermasculine figure that is impervious to disease or decay. Moral heroes perform every task with ease and resolve, without second-guessing or anxiety. This myth isn't new, but a long-lasting legacy of Greek heroes from Odysseus to Heracles. To be truly great is to be unquestionably independent, in full use of all bodily capacities, and living out one's wildest and most ambitious dreams. In this model, weakness and disability are genuinely bad, deficient, and defective forms of human existence. Vulnerability is the hallmark of decay and immorality. Moral champions renounce intimacy and interdependence in favor of radical independence. It is easier, of course, to drive past hitchhikers and shrug off the feeling that we are *torn* when we are independent and uncommitted.

These themes run deep in a variety of cultures, perhaps clearest in ancient Greek epics or American westerns. In these stories, Lone Ranger heroes ride into town and exert tremendous influence on others and then ride off into the sunset, unencumbered by relationships or commitments to the towns they just saved. The love interest, stereotypically feminine, stands at the town gate, tears in her eyes, waving good-bye to the "masked man." Such heroes, whether we find them cresting the next mountain ridge in the Wild West or riding a polished sports car into the Miami night, teach us that we are the most human when we need nothing and rely on nobody. Such heroes are complete; untorn, they need no "other" to give them life. They are "whole," with or without the neighbor.

One of the most famous lines in American film was delivered by Clint Eastwood in the now-classic 1983 movie *Sudden Impact*. Eastwood's character, officer Dirty Harry, witnesses a holdup at the diner where he is enjoying his morning coffee. The thief puts a gun to the head of a waitress and threatens to shoot her. Rather than backing down at the hostage situation, Harry pulls his own gun and aims it at the head of the gunman and growls, "Go ahead, make my day." The implication? Harry will exact instant and painful justice if the thief pulls the trigger. The criminal, along with the audience, is shocked. Aren't people supposed to be remarkably affected by the endangerment of innocent people? If the criminal shoots, Eastwood claims that his "day" will be made. One gets the impression that nothing that happens to anyone *else* has the potential of ruining his day. In this sense, Dirty Harry is repeating a familiar story we never tire of hearing. If you aspire to write movies or books, take careful notes; this stuff sells.

In the classical comedy *The Frogs* by the ancient Greek playwright Aristophanes, the shifty Dionysus, son of Zeus, is repeatedly shamed by his slave Xanthias. By all appearances, Xanthias is braver and wittier than his master. On more than one occasion, Dionysus begs Xanthias to exchange clothes with him to prevent risky confrontations. When Xanthias wears the divine garb of his master, he also wears a proverbial bull's-eye on his back. Dionysus had made a few enemies along with way. By swapping attire he was comically hiding from the consequences of his own actions and also showing himself to be less than worthy of his "divine" status.

At one point in the ancient play, because of the confusion of costume exchanges, a test is devised to determine which one of them is divine. The test is based on a typical and pervasive assumption about divinity in Hellenistic mythology and philosophy. Xanthias and Dionysus are both flogged and watched carefully to see who will first be caught "flinching or crying out." For, "If you can see any of us paying attention, or crying in pain at what you are doing, you'll know that one isn't a god."[2] To be divine, apparently, is to be impervious to the sting of a whip and pressure of thorns.

Xanthias proves repeatedly in *The Frogs* to act more divine than his supposedly godly master. The duel ends when Dionysus cries out and proclaims his birth-given status. But the cleverness of this comic play is found in the irony of a slave who acts more divine than a god. If there is a moral to the story of *The Frogs*, perhaps it is that Greek divinity is as much achieved as it is given. Not born divine, Xanthias manages to carry himself in a manner befitting of the Greek Olympians.

For both the Greek storytellers and the great philosophers of ancient Greece, the clearest mark of divinity may be the inability to suffer or fear. Dirty Harry would pass this test with flying colors. Despite being presented with a situation that would fill most people with sympathy and fear, he stands unfazed by the villain who can only make his "day" by giving Harry a chance to pull the trigger. Under Homer's pen we find countless stories that underscore the no-suffering criteria for godliness. The heroes Achilles and Odysseus are praised for being nearly gods in their ability to shrug off adversity, peril, and pain. Though both characters occasionally show compassion or weakness, their high accolades are a credit to their ultimate invulnerability. Suffering and vulnerability are the antitheses of divinity in both Greek philosophy and Greek mythology. Change and vulnerability are weak; permanence is divine.

Here we find ourselves grappling with a cherished and favorite story, a story that appears in thousands of forms and ropes us in repeatedly. Like the Greeks, we love to hear stories about heavily muscled heroes who stand unscathed by the forces of evil. Children are reared on cartoons and games underwritten by this story. Since stories shape human life and community in remarkable and vivid ways, I am quick to be critical of the ways the "impervious hero" story is harmful. In short, such narratives can lead to unhealthy understandings of personhood, gender, power, relationship, love, and justice, to name just a few. Still, this story is not all bad. These kinds of superman heroes often fly to the aid of the weak, bind the wounds of the broken, and take the side of the powerless underdog. They often arise from lowly beginnings, from poverty or freak accidents or alien life-capsules. It stirs the heart to see the hero battle against impossible odds and oppressive power and still carry a deep concern for the helpless and the needy. These heroes haven't led us down a completely dark alley. But they have left behind a deep and pervasive mythology and theology of wholeness, completeness, and invulnerability.

Even the most uneventful life is bound for some measure of sorrow and brokenness. If, somehow, we were able to avoid calamities and disease, and even if we are lucky enough to live in times of peace and in tranquil lands, degeneration and death await us all. We prefer not to think about death, and who could blame us? No amount of spiritual assurances can erase the looming trauma of death; even those with the deepest faith are torn in death.

Even Jesus? It would seem so. We are fortunate in this regard that the gospel of Luke takes pains to show how Jesus himself was torn in the garden of Gethsemane. Before he is arrested, Jesus spends hours struggling on his knees in prayer. While his disciples doze nearby, Jesus agonizes over his impending suffering and death, crying out that the cup of suffering be taken from him (22:42). Jesus' struggle is lonely, despite his requests for support from his friends. He is feeling his life "tear" as he looks at multiple futures and longs for one that does not include the pain that looms before him. Jesus is torn between his own will and the will of the Father to whom he prays. He prays, repeatedly, "not my will but yours" (v. 42). The prayers of Jesus before his death sound different from John's perspective, where Jesus faces down his execution with tranquility and confidence. Luke sees this night differently and seems interested in leaving behind a gut-wrenching, blood-sweating perspective on Jesus' night in the garden. The phrase recorded in Luke 22 is stunning: "And being in anguish, he prayed more earnestly, and his sweat was like drops of blood falling to the ground" (v. 44, NIV).[3] This verse appears as a strong testament to the relationship between authentic human life and the terror and trauma of brokenness. Jesus, too, was radically torn.

The tearing can be small and almost undetectable, as in the parting of good friends or the incremental approach of old age. The tearing can be bittersweet, like the tears I cried as my children walked up the stairs and through the big red door to kindergarten. The tearing can also cut us to the core, and never more than when we dare to love wholeheartedly. What is love if not a grand risk of being torn? The soaring heights of love are majestic, in all of love's manifestations, but to care is to put oneself in jeopardy. The Greek heroes are good at limiting their "care" for their friends and even their family. To care and to love is to be vulnerable. Odysseus had to forfeit the lives of every single member of his crew to survive his long journey home to Ithaca. It is better, then, to keep people around us at a distance. To love is to risk suffering. This sort of heroism seems like the exact opposite to what we see in Luke's description of Jesus on the night he was betrayed. Jesus is filled with apprehension, struggle, and anxiety. His prayers are not the prayers of Odysseus; his resolve is not the resolve of the Lone Ranger. Jesus' Gethsemane prayers portray him as vulnerable, incomplete, torn.

Perhaps this partly explains the depth of Jesus' anxiety in Gethsemane. He is anxious not just for himself and his death but also for those whose lives are bound up in his. He asks his disciples to pray, after all, not for his sake but for their own, that they might "not fall into temptation" (Luke 22:40, NIV). Sadly, only eight verses later Luke tells the story of Peter's temptation and betrayal. Jesus' suffering is commensurate with his love. When Luke reports that Jesus sweated drops of blood, his statement relates to the depth of Jesus' anxiety. Jesus was torn to the very degree that he loved. The option will always be available to us to love *less*. But this does not appear to be the alternative chosen by Jesus.

The mythology of completeness inhibits our ability to "mourn" for the responsibilities we are unable to fulfill. To be torn is to be human, and to be human is to be tempted to pretend that one is not torn. In the realm of morality, this means we are tempted to pretend we have been sufficiently responsible simply because we have met *one* of our competing obligations. If we are indeed more responsible than we can ever realize, and if we are to think of ourselves as obligated in an infinite manner, how are we to grapple with the inevitable tearing between multiple goods? When we have one cup of cold water to give and many are thirsty, how do we cope with the suffering felt by the ones who don't get a drop?

It starts, I think, with coming to grips with the fact that from stem to stern, human life is torn. Every choice is also a renunciation, a turning away from other choices. Death and loss are real, and we must not be numb to these aspects of reality. At an even deeper level, the fantasy of completeness leads to a negative and dismissive attitude toward the disabled, the elderly, the young, and everyone else who does not verify their worth with some form of usefulness. This divisive myth makes the pinnacle of human experience an unattainable and rare brand of strong and independent existence. All other stages of life, or manifestations of human existence, are by definition inferior.

But what if humanity's finest manifestation is visible in the vulnerability of Jesus in Gethsemane or in the quiet mourning of Mary and Mary beside his tomb? What if production and independence are misleading measures of human value and importance? The mythology of wholeness and completeness drives a social mentality that threatens responsibility on all sides. We may be tempted by this myth to think there is a spiritual good to being impervious to one's neighbor. We may also be tempted to think there is a pathway through life that is free of anxiety, mourning, suffering, or loss. But this pathway is a pure fiction. The aching of incomplete life can be subtle or obvious, but facing and embracing brokenness is a richly Christian, deeply human, practice.

The obsession with wholeness is also a driving force behind a rigid form of morality that seeks to draw firm lines between where responsibility begins and ends. In such a mindset, we cannot be whole if we are failing in ethical obligations, so it is imperative to know when we are morally upright and when we are morally suspect. This brand of subtle legalism must draw firm and steady lines to safeguard moral integrity. The pressure to draw lines carefully delineating the beginning and end of responsibility is related to the myth of wholeness and completion. How can I feel complete if I never know where my obligations end? But it is in this tension of unknowing that we must live; to be truly responsible is to forfeit the comfort that comes from the myth of wholeness.

Life is full of existential anxieties, the kind of maddening pressures that never seem to slacken. But perhaps the fact that we are torn should leave us *more* sensitive to the tensions we can't resolve along the roads of life. I cannot stop to help every hitchhiker, but that does not mean I should shun the impulse to mourn the tension inherent in my double responsibility. I fulfill one obligation and shirk another. It might be tempting to make this tension easier, to refuse to look in the rearview mirror and scramble my brain for a way to meet both obligations. But to move away from the place where I am torn is to move away from responsibility.

Until we can live in a world in which every hitchhiker can be helped, we must remain hungry and yearning. The longing for that world is a *holy* desire; we are trained to ignore and suppress it, but it is a desire for justice. This longing can be overwhelmed by legalism, by individualism, and by a host of myths that mute the infinite call for justice and hospitality. Listening to the quiet voices of others and the needs inherent in their plight leaves us remarkably torn. Too many people are thirsty, too many people are poor, and too many people are sick. The tension created by these pains makes us mindful that we are incomplete beings. And this ache of incompletion means we are wired for compassion, responsibility, and justice. But the dream of being complete dies a long and slow death.

Cain's unanswered question, to which we have returned regularly in this book, presumes the absurdity of responsibility. He cannot, of course, be everywhere his brother might wander. Cain cannot protect Abel from beasts and potholes and mosquitoes. Cain's deception is telling. He wonders, out loud, why should he be concerned over the welfare of his brother? His mocking exclamation, "Am I my brother's keeper?" (Gen. 4:9), speaks volumes about his understanding of humanity and the connection between his welfare and the welfare of his brother. He expects that until proven guilty of murder, he is *not* responsible for Abel's welfare.

But to be human is to be bound to sisters and brothers in a way that never allows us to break off the rearview mirror. Cain cannot be Abel's keeper, at least not in every sense of "keeping" him safe. But Cain can *mourn* his inability to do so. Perhaps if Cain thought in this way about his brother, the grandfather of all murders could have been prevented.

eleven

FAITH AND KNIVES

FAITH can be a marvel or a horror. Faith has guided some of the greatest triumphs of humankind, and faith has driven us into some of our deepest nightmares. It takes a powerful faith to stand up to the towering powers of racism, sexism, and oppression. A strange form of faith is also at work when people fly planes into buildings or detonate suicide bombs. In the end, faith may be humanity's greatest asset and most bitter curse. We can therefore hardly blame noisy atheists like Richard Dawkins for questioning the value of religion; every day religious faith is used to justify atrocious behavior around the world. An analysis of the role of faith is well worth our time in this exploration of human responsibility. After all, it requires a kind of radical faith to embrace the excessive form of responsibility advocated in this book. So what about faith?

In 1992, a twelve-year-old boy named Andrew Wantland was pronounced dead on arrival when an ambulance brought him to St. Jude Hospital in Orange County California.[1] Andrew had been a thriving young boy until just months before his death. Friends and family noticed that Andrew began to rapidly lose weight, that he developed a nagging cough, and that he seemed to be constantly drinking water. He missed some time from school with what his family called "the flu." In actuality, Andrew was beginning to manifest obvious symptoms of diabetes, an extremely common disease suffered by 8 percent of people living in the United States.[2] But his father, who had custody of Andrew, was involved with the Church of Christ, Scientist, which encourages members to shun medical interventions and seek healing through prayer, Bible reading, and other faith-based practices. Andrew's condition grew worse, even as his father, grandmother, and Christian Science practitioners prayed over him. Until just a few hours before his death, simple injections of insulin and fluids would have saved his life. In the United States there are thousands of children like Andrew with diabetes who continue to live relatively normal lives with the assistance of these lifesaving interventions. Andrew probably slipped into a coma well before he died, but even then his caretakers failed to get him emergency medical care. When he died, he had lost thirty-five pounds, his body decimated by a very treatable disease.[3]

The California courts found Andrew's father, grandmother, and the Church of Christ, Scientist, innocent of all charges. They were acting within the scope of their First Amendment religious freedoms, according to both the lower court and the appeals court. Judge William Bedsworth gave this statement to justify the court's decision to exonerate all parties of wrongdoing: "Imposing any duty upon Christian Science healers which require them to encourage patients to seek medical care would directly interfere with their own religious practices."[4]

We are justifiably appalled at Andrew's death and at the death of many other children in his situation. Our bodies and the bodies of our children are beset by a host of diseases and ailments that are readily treatable with the tools of modern medicine. Despite these tools, children under the care of Christian Scientist parents and guardians have died from blood poisoning, ruptured appendixes, infections, cancer, and a range of other illnesses.[5] We may also be disturbed by the decisions made by the California courts, which seem to leave children radically vulnerable to the dangerous faith of their parents. If Andrew's teacher, school nurse, or neighbor had whisked him to the hospital to save his life, without consent, would they have been prosecuted? These are important questions, but they are questions of legislation. For our purposes here, it should suffice to claim, without much controversy, that Andrew's family and church failed to be responsible for his welfare. Their failure cost him his life.

Sadly, we live in a world where children are regularly failed in large and small ways. What is particularly disturbing about this story is that Andrew was failed *in the name of faith*. Even more disturbing is the glut of biblical stories that might encourage parents to act in similar ways. We are caught between a rock and a hard place: radical responsibility requires deep faith, but faith is also routinely complicit in the most barbaric acts of irresponsibility. This chapter examines this complex relationship through the lens of one disturbing but central story in Christian and Jewish scripture.

The story of Abraham and Isaac, told in Gen. 22, is regularly correlated with these stories of children who died because of the faith of their parents. The story of Abraham's near-sacrifice of Isaac on Mount Moriah has been told and retold in countless manners. For our purposes here, we will focus on the retelling the story receives under the pen of Johannes de Silentio, one of the pseudonyms used by nineteenth-century Danish philosopher Søren Kierkegaard. In the famous book *Fear and Trembling*, Johannes ponders the story of Abraham's journey up the mountain. He has heard countless sermons on the passage, rehearsing the familiar call of Abraham to sacrifice Isaac and his faithful journey to the top of the mountain. In the common sermons, claims Johannes, the preacher pronounces Abraham the "father of faith" for being willing to give his utmost to God. The preacher then turns to the congregation and reminds them to give their best to God, and then everyone rushes home to Sunday dinner and a nice nap.[6]

Johannes does a double take, from the text to the sermon and back to the text. The actions of Abraham, in his estimation, bear little or no resemblance to the popular application. Abraham raised a knife above the body of his son! Johannes concludes that Abraham is either a monster or his faith is a marvel that transcends and obliterates the reasonable and prevalent definitions of faith. At face value, Abraham's behavior resembles acts we normally attribute to a lunatic. Hearing a voice of God, he brings a defenseless child to the top of a mountain and ties him up to kill him. These are grounds for conviction and imprisonment, perhaps with padded walls. How is this willingness to take the life of an innocent human a testament to faith? It sounds much more like evidence of delusion and instability.

It is this question that keeps Johannes, and presumably Kierkegaard, awake at night in "fear and trembling." Christians, Jews, and Muslims consider Abraham the "father of faith." But in this Genesis narrative Abraham looks more like the progenitor of domestic violence. Johannes launches into a series of reflections on Abraham, wondering all along what understanding of faith might help us make sense of this story. At stake throughout the work of Kierkegaard is a theme of significant importance in this book. What has *reason* to do with faith? In *Fear and Trembling* the core issue relates to ethics and responsibility. Abraham appears to act irresponsibly in this key passage of the book of Genesis. Should the calls to responsibility trump faith? Should faith be set aside in respect for the deep calls for extreme hospitality? Put simply, what does faith have to do with responsibility? Abraham is given the choice between being *faithful* to the command of God or *responsible* to the faces of his son and his wife. The choice he makes may be admirable to some, but to Johannes it seems just plain scary.

The struggle to align Abraham's actions with any rational conception of faith leads Johannes to narrate several alternative endings to Abraham's story. In each case, Abraham chooses a more reasonable and logical reaction to the horrible sacrifice that is asked of him. In one telling, he ignores the command and his family watches the faith die in his eyes. In another, he plunges the knife into his chest, much more willing to give his own life than to take another's. In yet another, Johannes imagines Abraham feverishly searching the bushes for a replacement sacrifice when he reaches the top of Moriah. Each of these alternatives provides a story that can be assimilated with our more reasonable understandings of faith.[7] But

Abraham takes none of these routes. He moves with resolution to the mountaintop and binds Isaac with the odd and horrific faith to which no honest modern person could relate. Could I emulate Abraham's act of faith? I hope not.

So should we advocate a form of reasonable responsibility that eliminates faith because we have found something better and higher? Is the reasoning of morality our new deity? Johannes suspects that Abraham lives in a place that is utterly foreign to the realm of reasonable responsibility. The story does not end with Isaac's death, after all, but with Isaac being returned to Abraham. Walking down Mount Moriah, Abraham "has" Isaac in a radically different way than if he had stayed home and ignored God's call. Isaac is the beloved that comes to him as a pure gift from God—twice over. The deepest desires of his heart are realized, and he has proven that he puts nothing above his allegiance to God. So noting that Abraham doesn't kill Isaac, and setting aside the legitimate question about what kind of God would test a man like this, Johannes focuses his attention on Abraham's glorious life. Abraham's dreams are fulfilled, but completely without selfishness. He has given up everything, and somehow still has everything. How can we not envy the place where he lives? Dubbing Abraham a "Knight of Faith," Johannes admires him from afar. As desperately as we may struggle to understand Abraham, he seems to live in a land far away. His faith is too radical, too abrupt, too dangerous, and it seems to suspend ethics.

To his credit, Kierkegaard does not allow his pseudonym to resolve this tension but leaves the reader to ask this question anew. I have appealed throughout this book to biblical wisdom and a form of responsibility that arises from Christian and Jewish scripture. But does this understanding of responsibility arise out of Judeo-Christianity only to sever itself from faith altogether? This would be troubling, since the sort of responsibility advocated here certainly challenges and defies anything that can be derived from logic alone. It takes *faith* to craft cities of refuge, care for Judas, guard the boundaries of *Hakeldema,* lay down the rights and riches, or resist the temptation of Gyges.

To answer this pressing question it may be worth spending some concerted attention on Gen. 22. We must agree with Johannes that this text is generally hijacked and watered down to mean almost nothing. The story is jarring and alarming; only a blatantly unfaithful reading of this text can correlate Abraham's sacrifice with anything that sits easy over Sunday dinner. We may not lay awake at night worrying about the theological and ethical implications of this passage, but Johannes should at least leave us convinced that this passage needs to be left alone or taken seriously. The middle ground, which distorts and dilutes the horror of Abraham's predicament, must be eliminated. Abraham is either a hero of faith or a lunatic who narrowly avoids an atrocious murder. For our purposes here we will track along with Johannes a little further, in hopes there is something about Abrahamic faith that leads us *toward* and not *away from* responsibility.

The phenomenon that is child sacrifice is one of the most perplexing and disturbing issues in human history. For reasons that require careful analysis, cultures around the globe practiced the heinous act of child sacrifice with some regularity over the course of human history. We can see instances of child sacrifice written into the fabric of dozens of ancient cultures, from ancient Europe, Asia, Africa, the Americas, and the Middle East. How could people from such diverse societies commit this common act of ritualized killing? The answer may lie in a general theological suspicion that the gods will require the very best and most precious gifts that people can offer. In ancient societies, and hopefully modern ones as well, the most precious resource was children. Far more than land or money, most ancient cultures prized progeny. To have many children, often sons in particular, was to be truly rich. The sacrifice of animals and money to earn divine approval was most common. But on some occasions there would arise a dire need to awaken or arouse the energy of a deity who demanded the highest possible sacrifice. Terrified by impending war, poor crops, drought, or disease, people needed to prove to their gods that they desperately warranted assistance. We are justified, of course, in wondering whether "faith" is the proper word for this behavior. But it is hard to deny that there is a kind of foolish faith found in this horrific willingness to slay even children on the altar.

Abraham's story is not the only time child sacrifice becomes an issue in the Hebrew Bible. In what may be the most disturbing narrative in Christian and Jewish scripture, Judg. 11 tells the story of Jephthah, who cries out for help on the battlefield when hope of victory seems to be lost. To prove the depth of his faith, and to warrant the assistance of God in his moment of dire need, Jephthah promises to sacrifice "whoever comes out of the doors of [his] house to meet [him]" (v. 31) if God helps him defeat his enemy. Sure enough, Jephthah's troops rally and win the battle. Back home, it is Jephthah's daughter who first walks through his door, and he feels that he must keep his promise to God by killing her on the altar "as a burnt offering" (v. 31). She is given a little time to mourn the loss of her own future and dies beneath Jephthah's blade.[8] The contrast with Abraham's story is stark; Isaac lives, but Jephthah's child is killed and burnt as an offering to the same God. For that matter, the families of children like Andrew Wantland should be counted on the same ledger. One can hardly call these people cowardly, even if we judge them deeply misguided.

Abraham, Jephthah, and Andrew Wantland's church and family share a common willingness to act *irresponsibly* for God's sake. It seems that in each of these cases there was a common presumption that their deity *might* ask them to make this horrific sacrifice. Abraham and Jephthah at least lived in a culture where this kind of sacrifice was occasionally practiced. But something different happened on Mount Moriah, something Jephthah, whose story occurs generations after Abraham, would have been wise to remember.

The Genesis text indicates that Abraham was looking down at Isaac, knife held high, when he heard the angel's voice telling him not to harm the boy (22:12). The direction of Abraham's gaze is significant; the commandment to *not murder* speaks to Abraham as he looks at the face of Isaac, his beloved. Abraham learns an invaluable, historic lesson on Mount Moriah: to have faith in this God is to heed the "do not kill me" written in the face of the other. The significance of this lesson is far-reaching.

Johannes focused his reflections on this passage at the level of Abraham's willingness to climb that mountain and commit this heinous act as proof of the depth of his faith. But for our purposes here, we are justified in asking, how does faith function *after* Abraham? As Abraham packs his belongings and heads down the mountain from Moriah, what has Israel learned about faith? Does this story confirm or condemn the willingness to sacrifice children? For Johannes, Abraham teaches us that faith can sometimes suspend, or surpass, the realm of responsibility. But I wonder if there isn't something even richer to be identified in the moment when Abraham's knife is raised.

Abraham brings to the mountain two distinct heritages that make up the backbone of ancient Hebrew religion: responsibility and faith. These two commitments often work together, as we have seen in the legislation of Jubilee, the cities of refuge, the concern for widows and orphans, and in countless other instances. But there is also a question about whether they might occasionally work in opposition. Does faith, at least sometimes, require that we act irresponsibly, that we disregard the needs and bodies of others to show our allegiance to God?

The answer at Moriah is *no*. Abraham's experience on Moriah united the best in faith with the best in morality. Faith may require seemingly foolish levels of responsibility and require that believers go to extreme and unreasonable lengths for the sake of justice. But faith in this God does not, hereafter, mean violating the lives and bodies of others. To be sure, this lesson was not quickly or easily learned. Jephthah's tragic folly is testament to the reluctance of ancient Israel to learn this lesson. Psalm 137, which celebrates the bashing death of Babylonian infants, emblemizes the failure to learn the lesson of Moriah.[9] One may justifiably wonder whether Abraham's lesson has been learned even today, given the way "faith" leads some "Christian" groups to treat Muslims, Jews, homosexuals, immigrants, and many others.

What happens on Mount Moriah is a fusion between faith and responsibility. The foolishness of faith is surely retained;

in what other mode than faith can we receive and care for the extreme pain of the world? It takes radical, foolish faith to attempt the form of responsibility advocated in this book and in the teachings of Jesus. It is only in the mode of faith that Christians walk the second mile, turn the other cheek, and dare to love even enemies (see Matt. 5:43-48). Only faith, not logic or reason, pushes Christians into the margins of the world where the poorest of the poor need more than charity to turn around their lives. Only faith scours the world's ditches, like the Good Samaritan, in search of the broken bodies who have been crushed beneath the heel of selfishness and greed. Logic and reason can produce charity and even great generosity. But Christian responsibility goes much further. And this "further" is faith.

After Moriah, faith in God can no longer drive us to sacrifice others on the altar of our own agendas. When our knives are raised, as was the case with both Abraham and Jephthah, the faces of others should arrest our movement toward violence. It is through the face of Isaac that Abraham is to find an everlasting message about religion and religious responsibility. To love God is to love the neighbor.

This conclusion should not seem shocking for Christians familiar with Jesus' fusion of what he considered the two great commandments. Pressed to name the most important of the commandments, Jesus refused, citing *two* commandments instead of one. And the commandments he selected confirm our suspicion on Mount Moriah. The great commandments are, of course, to love God and to love neighbor. But even more intriguing is the "hook" with which Jesus connects the two commands. After saying the first great commandment is to love God with all your heart, soul, and mind, he says the second commandment "is like it" (Matt. 22:39).[10] How are these commandments, to love God and to love neighbor, similar to one another? After Moriah, the face of the other person must always be understood to bear the trace of God, the voice that calls out from on high, "Do not murder me."

Ironically, the transcendence of God appears in the frailty and complexity of the human face. And the face of the other, as Jesus makes clear in his "least of these" parable in Matt. 25, is not just the face of the innocent child but also the face of the sick, lonely, hungry, and poor. Even more starkly, Jesus claims that whenever we have failed to visit the criminal in prison, who has probably earned a place behind prison bars, we fail to visit Jesus himself. The fusion, in Jesus, is complete. To love God is to love the other. To have faith in *this* God is to be concerned for the welfare of the sick, the hungry, the manslayer, the murderer, the oppressed, the widow, and the orphan.

But this is a fusion of faith and responsibility that is easily forgotten, easily submerged beneath panicky concerns for self-preservation, denominational differences, and disembodied evangelism. From the Abraham story we must simply reject any application that might leave us raising knives over the defenseless, or denying penicillin or insulin to ailing children. These cannot be the legacy of Abraham or the role of faith in the world today. But retained from the Abraham narrative must be the insistence that faith exceeds and defies the confines of what we are inclined to find reasonable. After Abraham's arm is arrested in midair, we need not worry that faith beckons us to murder. The radical nature of Christian faith operates in the reverse, operating irrationally on behalf Isaac, the poor, the other, the neighbor, and even the enemy. The narrative from Mount Moriah fuses radical faith with radical responsibility. This story should read as a condemnation to Jephthah and to anyone else who drops the knife, failing to hear the voice saying, "Do not lay your hand on the boy" (Gen. 22:12).

Also retained from Abraham and his experiences on Moriah is the mystery of *joy*. One could easily see a recipe for somber unhappiness in the radical responsibility advocated throughout this text and throughout Christian and Jewish scripture. But Abraham is no somber zombie of obedience. His act of faith coincides with a hope in happiness, despite the irony of that hope. People who give themselves over to lives of deep responsibility cannot lose sight of the abundant life that occurs within the context of such living. His obedience is neither miserable nor glum. Abraham willingly forfeits his own happiness but somehow never loses sight of the fact that this forfeiture does not mean he will never be happy. What it does mean is that his joy will be a *gift*, not something he retains by holding on tightly.

If anything, the story of Abraham underscores the need for faith in the realm of responsibility. For Abraham to not harm Isaac is one form of responsibility. But this is probably better described as avoiding irresponsibility. But if anything is clear from the preceding chapters of this book, it is that the concept of responsibility is much richer than merely avoiding immoral behavior. To be responsible to Isaac is to hear the "thou shalt not murder" written on the face of every Isaac. To live by faith is to be keeper of the other, but not just by laying down our knives. To endeavor to reverse Cain's course and be Abel's keeper is truly to embrace an obligation that is nothing short of scandalous.

twelve

INCONCLUSION

THERE IS SOMETHING irresistible about stories. With my kids tucked into their covers each night I find myself spinning tales or enjoying the retelling of stories older than recorded history. Their minds whirl, not always toward sleep, as I narrate the journeys of knights and unicorns, tortoises and hares, princesses and castles. Sometimes, long after I think they are asleep, one of them will whisper, "Dad, are there really such things as magic carpets?" The imaginations of children are wondrous as they go on nightly journeys into books and fictional lands where anything is possible. Sometimes I will crack open a dusty copy of Grimm's Fairy Tales or a book of Greek, Chinese, or Indian mythology. One night as I read to them from Jack London's classic novel *White Fang,* my mind wandered. I was reading about one of White Fang's cruel owners, who beat him nearly to death, but I was inattentive to my words and their impact on my audience. My mind snapped out of a fog at the sound of two sobbing children, mourning the fictional beating of the poor wolf. I hurried to wrench the narrative back into a realm more conducive to happy dreams and sleepy children.

Stories, if well told, are rich, diverse, and illuminating. They may also be scary. I routinely find myself editing the stories to better suit the imaginations of my children and their need for imminent, nightmare-free sleep. Perhaps one needs only read such stories to children to realize how often our favorite stories include alarming acts of violence and cruelty. Stories inside and outside of Christian scripture routinely include the removal of heads, the mutilation of bodies, and the threat of violence. Parents like me regularly gloss the violence of ancient tales as we recount them to our children. There is seemingly little to be gained from children hearing about the threat of cannibalism in the older versions of "Hansel and Gretel" and "Sleeping Beauty." So we strip the stories of violent plotlines and sexual nuance.

Bible stories are often ill suited for peaceful dreams; who dreams well after hearing about David's treatment of Goliath's corpse, Jephthah's execution of his daughter, or the story of Lot being raped by his own daughters? We edit, at least for our children, and we do so for very good reasons. Not every story is a good bedtime story, and not every Bible passage, for that matter, translates easily into modern application. So we gain a tremendous skill for exercising reason and exorcising the illogical and offensive elements of the stories we tell. I have become adept in this art, deftly redacting tales as I read them to my children, smoothly eliminating sexism, racism, and violence from my narrations.

As we turn to the final pages of this book, we must address the harrowing calls to responsibility brought forward in these chapters. In many cases, the call to responsibility seems as unreasonable and offensive as any other story, biblical or otherwise. The very insinuation that responsibility exceeds understanding is a kind of horrifying prospect. We are understandably inclined to cushion the impact of these claims. Responsibility, as it has been described here, is an expansive reality; it shifts and grows without regard to our resources. Responsibility, I have argued, is literally uncontainable. There is a justifiable impulse to reduce these extreme obligations to something more manageable and reasonable. We do this, routinely, with many passages of Scripture, let alone secular themes and stories. Why not here?

The eternal temptation, when it comes to responsibility, is the allure of *fairness*. The kind of responsibility advocated here is profoundly *unfair*. To embrace responsibility is to enter into an asymmetrical relationship with others, accepting responsibility for pain, hunger, and poverty that we did not cause. It means turning away from the comforts of despondency, despite all the compelling reasons to retreat into isolation. The implications are stark: responsibility of this sort requires that we consider the other to be greater than ourselves. How can people be expected to leave this kind of teaching unedited? Must we not blunt such a claim to protect ourselves from its awkward implications?

It seems, however, that the extreme nature of hospitality and responsibility is written into the fabric of the Christian gospel. Paul told the Philippians, stunningly, "regard others as better than yourselves" (2:3). Paul then illustrates his point by quoting what may be the earliest recorded Christian hymn. To consider others better than oneself, apparently, is to follow the example of Christ, who "emptied himself" (v. 7) and humbly accepted a death that should not have been his lot. In this central passage of Paul's letter to Philippi, he locates the elevation of the other at the center of Christian life. To be

Christian is to consider others better than oneself and then to incarnate this mind-set in sacrifices similar to those made by Christ, who was "obedient to the point of death" (v. 8). This hardly seems like a peripheral concept; the offensive nature of hyperbolic responsibility is written into this supremely central fabric of Christianity.

And here we may forgive Cain for his comment, if not his murder. His cry might be a reasonable one, were not his brother's blood still staining his hands. There is nothing reasonable about playing "keeper" to one's brothers and sisters and enemies. But this seems to be the offense of the Christian gospel. Is there some manner whereby we can soften Jesus' commandment to "love your enemies" (Matt. 5:44)? Surely people have tried; Christians have loved their enemies *to death* for many centuries. But Jesus, in the same sermon, illustrated what it means to love enemies. We are to turn another cheek when enemies strike (v. 39). We are commanded to walk a second mile when one mile is demanded of us (v. 41). We are to give away our coat when someone asks for a shirt (v. 40). The Sermon on the Mount is loaded with these grinding, offensive claims for Christian behavior in an eye-for-an-eye world. Jesus' preaching makes it impossible for us to set aside the extreme nature of responsibility for a more reasonable version. If anything, these teachings are permanently offensive. Who can fulfill his commandment that we "give to everyone who begs from you, and do not refuse anyone who wants to borrow from you" (v. 42)? Christians looking for reasonable expectations should avert their eyes from Matt. 5—7.

What we have seen in the parable of the Good Samaritan or in the parable of the sheep and the goats is a kind of responsibility that defies quantification and refuses to be confined. Responsibility moves like water around the bars we erect to confine it. We are responsible, it seems, when we least expect it and sometimes when we most want to be excused from the situation. And the ultimate illustration for this brand of responsibility comes through the centerpiece of the Christian gospel and the story of Jesus' passion. Christians have disagreed notoriously over the meaning and significance of the narratives describing Jesus' death and resurrection; yet however we interpret the story of the sacrifice of Jesus, Christianity has uniformly claimed that his sacrifice represents an embrace of unwarranted responsibility. Christians claim that in the death of Jesus Christ, God takes responsibility for the pain, suffering, and sin of the world. The centerpiece of the Christian story is a narrative about extreme, unreasonable responsibility.

This book has taken various angles on the question of responsibility, arguing for extreme responsibility from religious texts and from the everyday phenomenon of face-to-face encounters with suffering. Some readers will inevitably find some arguments more compelling than others. It should be pointed out that the results of these chapters remain *inconclusive*. Even if the reader is convinced that responsibility is dynamic and uncontainable, the question rears immediately: "*How* can we be responsible in a complex and broken world?"

The fact that we are unreasonably obligated to address suffering wherever it may be found does not imply any particular answer to that suffering. We cannot, for instance, expect to overcome poverty by sheer force of extreme charity. Poverty is a complex and insidious mechanism. Its resolution is not found by simply increasing the generosity of the rich. Truly addressing the needs of people in underdeveloped countries means *listening* for ways that a few tools, or a small loan, can help a dollar-a-day farmer make five dollars per day, and then fifty. At times we must address poverty with patience and caution, for generosity can sometimes do more harm than good. At other times we must fight poverty with reckless abandon. The nature of responsibility pivots on the face-to-face relation, on the infinite needs of those who suffer, whatever the cause. To ground responsibility is awkward, locating the core of *my* being within the perplexing and mysterious world of the other person.

Much has been said here about the discomforts of responsibility, and too little about the potential joys and wonders of this way of being in the world. This emphasis is intentional but unfortunate. Responsibility may *seem* like a burden, but it is also a potential source of life, healing, joy, and happiness. Ironically, being bound to one's neighbor provides a unique kind of freedom. The other person breaks me free from my past, from the future I might anticipate, from the prison of my private world. Responsibility, rooted in the primitive choice to *respond* is not merely about obligation. Responsibility is also liberation. The other person brings to me a future that is impossible without her, a past reconfigured by his presence in my world. The liberation provided by the other can be cause for great joy. Bound to the neighbor in responsibility, I find that her pains are my pains. But her joys are also my joys. In a completely real sense, the future of the other is my future; his life is my life. There are no guarantees in this realm of responsibility, but there are reasons to hope it might be full of life and joy.

Actively taking responsibility means releasing the need to comprehend how suffering can be alleviated or resolved. At times it means rigorous labor; at other times it means nothing more than a listening and patient ear. We must be wary of simple solutions to complicated problems and embracing the call for creative and sensitive approaches to poverty, violence, and suffering. In the face of limitless suffering, the simpler solutions attempt to resolve these situations with arm's-length charity or impatient violence. There will be a steady stream of good reasons to embrace these tools. However, both charity and violence solve the problem of suffering too quickly and easily; both stop short of true responsibility, and too often, both of these tools cause more suffering than they alleviate.

If anything, this book has relentlessly pointed to the truly impossible scope of Christian responsibility. Christians are responsible, I have argued, to a degree that exceeds all human capacity for responsible action. This incapacity is both a curse and a blessing. As a blessing such responsibility redeems me from myself, opening me to the joy and forgiveness that can never be achieved or earned. As a curse it can lead to unrelenting guilt. I have argued here that the Bible presents wave after wave of calls to unreasonable responsibility. This bombardment can strip readers of every hope that we may achieve biblical *goodness*. Furthermore, this overwhelming guilt can often result from the impossibility of meeting every possible need presented by the faces of so many neighbors. Guilt can be a truly overwhelming and debilitating emotion, and the psychological experience of guilt is often unhealthy. Even if we can cope with our inability to live up to some biblical standard for goodness, how can we cope with the guilt that seems to go hand in hand with love and responsibility? Working parents feel guilt for the time they miss with their children. Many people carry endless guilt for actions they have committed in the past, haunted by the knowledge of the lasting pain they have inflicted on others. I have argued forcibly here for overwhelming responsibility, but I am not confident that overwhelming *guilt* is much good to either God or neighbor.

So perhaps it is helpful to remember Kierkegaard's suggestion that we are all sick, all caught in the endless cycle of trying to be something we cannot ever be.[1] This sickness can lead to different kinds of despair. We can despair in a way that leads to death, or despair in a way that leads to life. The despair that leads to life acknowledges the hopelessness of being *good* and embraces instead the goodness that comes only as a gift from God. The only answer to despair is grace. In the face of overwhelming responsibility, and perhaps guilt, the appearance of grace is the only relief from an unbearable burden. Grace is not the slackening of responsibility, but the miracle of a forgiveness that is not forged from internal goodness or achievement. Nobody is responsible enough to be good. I wonder if perhaps this is some relief to the person whose guilt has become debilitating. To face down impossible responsibility is to be human and to be honest about one's situation. Paul, reflecting on his most majestic and earnest attempts to be righteous, counts them all rubbish, and Bible scholars tell us that the word Paul used there is too crass for literal translation (see Phil. 3:8). Goodness cannot be achieved; our best attempts are still soiled.

Yet forgiveness appears, from God and from neighbor. Goodness happens, interrupting our expectations and guilt. Sometimes churches welcome the wandering manslayer, we stop like the Samaritan and help the wounded person in the ditch, and justice rolls. In these moments we glimpse the appearance of grace, the event that is holiness. Grace is the possibility of happiness and joy, which are received as gifts and not as rights. Guilt is only the final answer and result of responsibility if this story is still about *me*, if I remain the protagonist in the narrative of my encounter with the other and with the world. Responsibility, however, has robbed me of my role as the main character in this story. I am first and foremost responsible, *keeper* of my sister and my brother. And as such I receive not just responsibility and suffering but also forgiveness and joy.

To despair is to be human; to despair toward life is to despair of my role as protagonist in this story of life and embrace the joy and forgiveness that are gifts from the other into whose story I find myself grafted. This is no magic formula to address the problem of guilt, but it points beyond any obsession with my own inadequacy and toward the grace of forgiveness and joy that arise as gifts from God and neighbor. To despair toward life is to be acutely aware of one's need for such gifts. Perhaps the overwhelming and scandalous nature of Christian responsibility is itself a gift, guiding me past both my ignorance and my fixation on my own story and its merits.

So we have reached an "inconclusion" to our journey, but perhaps that is what we might most expect from a book about responsibility. Our journey leads us out from the comfortable "home" of quantified responsibility in the same way Abram is called away from his homeland in Genesis. He is called to leave behind the familiar luxury of home and family and to go on a permanent journey that will not wind its way back home. By contrast, Odysseus, the hero of Homer's *Odyssey*, sets out on a long journey and fights his way back home. Against all odds and adversaries, Odysseus struggles to restore the life stripped from him by war and the will of the gods. But Abram is first renamed Abraham and then made to wander away from home, never to return. Odysseus is the undeniable protagonist in the story of the Odyssey; Abraham becomes a character in the story of God.

The resolution of Abraham's journey, I like to think, is yet to come. His journey moves toward reconciliation, toward forgiveness, and toward justice. Yet we live in a world where this future seems decidedly elusive, even impossible. The difference between the voyages of Odysseus and Abraham are significant in this regard. Odysseus must find his way home by his own vision and clever schemes. Odysseus sacrifices his neighbors, his crew, to safeguard his journey home. No one who departed with him from his homeland returned with him alive. They are all sacrificed at the altar of the protagonist, the need of the hero to have a happy ending. Abraham, on the other hand, is called to forfeit his right to a happy ending. He must simply give himself over, completely, to the future that is only his as pure gift. If anything, this book invites the reader into this second kind of voyage, the one that forfeits the role of protagonist along with the return trip. The story of the other takes priority: the stranger in the ditch, the alien at the gate, the hungry wanderer, the least of these.

As an invitation to this kind of journey, this book now arrives less at an end than at a beginning.

NOTES

Preface

1. This analogy is borrowed from Søren Kierkegaard, who suggests that God's Word is intended to function like a mirror. Kierkegaard, *For Self-Examination*, trans. Walter Lowrie (Oxford: Oxford University Press, 1941), 50.

2. Fyodor Dostoyevsky, *Brothers Karamazov* (New York: Signet Classic, 1999), 237.

3. Søren Kierkegaard, *The Sickness unto Death* (Princeton: Princeton University Press, 1980), 13-21.

4. "In the course of time Cain brought to the LORD an offering of the fruit of the ground, and Abel for his part brought of the firstlings of his flock, their fat portions. And the LORD had regard for Abel and his offering, but for Cain and his offering he had no regard. So Cain was very angry, and his countenance fell" (Gen. 4:3-5, NRSV).

Chapter 1

1. Liz Robbins, "Woman Who Lost Her Left Leg in Bus Accident Awarded $27.5 Million," *New York Times*, April 17, 2009. The court decision about the man injured by the subway train was later overturned by another judge.

2. Tetanus has been all but eradicated in industrialized countries thanks to relatively inexpensive vaccines that are readily available. But in nonindustrialized countries this potentially lethal disease strikes hundreds of thousands of people each year.

3. The immortalized words of defense attorney Johnny Cochran in his closing arguments at the famous O. J. Simpson trial.

4. "Ustinov's Comic Touch," BBC News, March 29, 2004, http://news.bbc.co.uk/2/hi/entertainment/3578959.stm (accessed January 3, 2011).

Chapter 2

1. Plato, *The Republic*, trans. Benjamin Jowett (Project Gutenberg, 2008), http://www.gutenberg.org/ebooks/1497.

2. Interesting advances in technology are allowing scientists to develop a rough version of an "invisibility cloak."

3. A note on Gen. 25:26 in the *New Oxford Annotated Bible: New Revised Standard Version*, reads: "*Jacob* is interpreted by a play on the Hebrew word for 'heel,' i.e. 'he takes by the heel' or 'he supplants.'" Bruce Metzger and Roland Murphy, eds., *The New Oxford Annotated Bible: New Revised Standard Version* (New York: Oxford University Press, 1991).

4. Kevin Danaher and Jason Mark, *Insurrection* (New York: Routledge, 2003), 95.

5. Ibid., 102.

6. Marc Gunther, "How Companies Fight Sweatshops," *Fortune Magazine*, May 2006.

7. Jan Kay, "Toxic Toys: San Francisco prepares to ban certain chemicals in products for kids, but enforcement will be tough—and toymakers question necessity," *San Francisco Chronicle*, November 19, 2006.

Chapter 3

1. Donald A. Grinde and Bruce E. Johansen, *Exemplars of Liberty: Native America and the Evolution of Democracy* (Los Angeles: University of California, 1991), 88.

2. Sherry Marker, *Plains Indian Wars* (New York: Infobase Publishing, 2003), 50.

3. Katie Kane, "Nits Make Lice," *Cultural Critique* 42 (Spring 1999): 81-103 (emphasis added).

4. U.S. Constitution, art. 1, sec. 2, cl. 3.

5. David Hume, "Of National Characters" (1748), in *The Philosophical Works*, ed. Thomas Hill Green and Thomas Hodge Grose (London, 1882; repr., Aalen: Scientia Verlag, 1964).

6. Immanuel Kant, *Observations on the Feeling of the Beautiful and the Sublime*, trans. J. T. Goldthwait (1763; Berkeley, Calif.: University of California Press, 1960).

7. This litany of quotations is found in Ella Shohat and Robert Stam, *Unthinking Eurocentrism* (New York: Routlege, 1994), 88.

8. United States Holocaust Memorial Museum, "Anti-Jewish Legislation in Prewar Germany," *Holocaust Encyclopedia*, http://www.ushmm.org/wlc/en/article.php?ModuleId=10005681 (accessed December 7, 2010).

9. Martin Luther, *On the Jews and Their Lies*, trans. Martin H. Bertram, in *Luther Works* (Philadelphia: Fortress Press, 1971), 47:137-42.

10. Ibid.

11. Ibid.

12. Stanley Arthur Cook, *The Laws of Moses and the Code of Hammurabi* (1903), 275: "Laws relating to the protection of slaves and animals from cruelty or injury . . . are more probably framed with the intent to ensure their protection as property, whereas in the Hebrew legislation the analogous injunctions spring rather from feelings of pure kindness."

Chapter 4

1. Hasbro recently sold a toy named the Zoids Gun Sniper.

2. "From the start Christianity was, essentially and fundamentally, the embodiment of disgust and antipathy for life, merely disguised, concealed, got up as the belief in an 'other' or a 'better life.'" Friedrich Nietzsche, *Attempt at a Self-Criticism* (1886; Penguin Classics, 1994), 9.

3. Daniel Ahern, *Nietzche As Cultural Physician* (University Park, Pa.: Pennsylvania State University Press, 1995), 127-29.

4. J. K. Rowling, *Harry Potter and the Sorcerer's Stone* (New York: Scholastic Press, 1998), 291.

5. The seventieth anniversary (U.S.) edition of Monopoly comes with a pamphlet in which Hasbro claims that more than 750 million people have played the game since its 1935 patent.

6. Dostoyevsky, *Brothers Karamazov*, 237.

Chapter 5

1. Deuteronomy 19:1-7 describes the problem related to the "hot anger" (v. 6) of a blood avenger, which might make him blind to the need for a just trial.

2. James Q. Wilson, *The Moral Sense* (New York: Simon and Shuster, 1997), 17.

3. Much thanks to Bible scholar Jeffrey Stackert for many of the insights in this chapter about biblical asylum.

4. This is one of the examples pondered in the Babylonian Talmud, Tract Maccoth, vol. 9, chap. 2, trans. Michael L. Rodkinson (1918), http://www.sacred-texts.com/jud/t09/mac07.htm.

5. Joshua 20 seems to tell the story of these cities being established, but beyond the report that the cities were established nothing more is offered. We are left to wonder about the effectiveness of this legislation in protecting manslayers.

6. Babylonian Talmud, Tract Maccoth, vol. 9, chap. 2. "Neither snares (for catching beasts) nor rope factories must there be established. All this is to prevent the relatives from coming to the cities of question."

7. Mircea Eliade, *The Sacred and the Profane: The Nature of Religion* (Orlando, Fla.: Harcourt, 1987), 20 ff.

8. For the Pentateuchal priestly authors, the Tent of Meeting—the divine abode—dwells in the center of the Israelite wilderness camp (see, e.g., Num. 1:50-53; 2:17).

9. Piotr Bienkowski and A. R. Millard, eds., *Dictionary of the Ancient Near East* (Philadelphia: University of Pennsylvania Press, 2000), 81-82. For biblical references to chaos (monsters) and the watery abyss, see, for example, Gen. 1:2; Isa. 51:10; 63:13; Ezek. 26:19; Jonah 2:6; Pss. 74:13-14; 77:17; 104:5-9; Job 9:18; 26:12.

10. See Num. 35:9-34.

11. United States Congress, *Oversight of the United States Sentencing Commission* (Washington, D.C.: U.S. G.P.O., 2001), 93.

12. Numbers 35 prescribes that this time of house arrest is to last until the current high priest dies.

Chapter 6

1. Associated Press, "Barnett: 'I can't live their lives for them,'" ESPN, April 14, 2004, http://sports.espn.go.com/ncf/news/story?id=1781123.

2. Lee Jenkins, "Losses Do to Barnett What Colorado Scandal Could Not," *New York Times*, December 9, 2005, http://www.nytimes.com/2005/12/09/sports/ncaafootball/09colorado.ready.html.

3. Ibid.

4. Babylonian Talmud, Tract Maccoth, vol. 9, chap. 2.

5. Emmanuel Levinas, *Beyond the Verse: Talmudic Readings and Lectures* (Bloomington, Ind.: Indiana University Press, 1994), 43.

6. Curiously, though Num. 35:11 describes the manslayer's action as "in error/unintentional" (*bishgagah*), there is no corresponding purification offering prescribed, as might be expected in light of Lev. 4. Homicide seems to fall outside of the sacrificial system of atonement, requiring the death of the high priest for restitution/expiation (cf. Num. 35:25, 28).

7. John Wesley, "Salvation by Faith," *The Bicentennial Edition of the Works of John Wesley* (Nashville: Abingdon Press, 1983—), 1:124.

8. John Wesley, *A Plain Account of Christian Perfection* (Kansas City: Beacon Hill Press, 1966).

9. Levinas, *Beyond the Verse*, 43.

10. Ibid., 188.

11. Graham Hays, "Central Washington offers the ultimate act of sportsmanship," ESPN.com, http://sports.espn.go.com/ncaa/columns/story?id=3372631 (accessed December 8, 2010).

Chapter 7

1. The Greek here uses the word μεταμεληθεις, literally "having regretted (it)."

2. This narrative, critical to this chapter, is found in Matt. 27:3-10.

3. Luke 22:3: "Satan entered into Judas"; John 13:2: "The devil had already put it in the heart of Judas son of Simon Iscariot to betray him."

4. In verse 23, Jesus quotes Ps. 41:9.

5. Certainly this is more ambiguous and nuanced than the attribution of Judas's betrayal to satanic possession in Luke 22:3.

6. In Deut. 23:18 the ill-gotten gains are from prostitution.

7. Donald Hagner, *Word Biblical Commentary: Matthew 14–28* (Dallas: Word Books, 1995), 813.

8. The Aramaic name apparently stuck to this piece of land; in verse 8, Matthew claims that the same plot is called *Hakeldema* "to this day."

9. Lisa W. Foderaro, "Private Moment Made Public, Then a Fatal Jump," *New York Times*, September 30, 2010.

10. Though the purchase of the field is found in Jer. 32, the context for this transaction is most clear in chapter 37, when Jeremiah is, ironically, accused of planning to desert to the encroaching enemy (vv. 13-14).

Chapter 8

1. Barbara Perry, *Hate and Bias Crime: A Reader* (New York: Routledge, 2003), 183-84.

2. René Girard, *Violence and the Sacred* (New York: Continuum, 2005), 8. Girard succinctly defines the mechanism when he describes one incidence as "a deliberate act of collective substitution performed at the expense of a victim and absorbing all the internal tensions, feuds, and rivalries pent up within the community."

3. René Girard, *Things Hidden Since the Foundation of the World* (New York: Continuum, 2003), 224 ff.

4. James Outman and Elizabeth Outman, *Terrorism: Almanac* (Farmington Hills, Mich.: U*X*L, 2002), 156.

5. Lori Lee Wilson, *The Salem Witch Trials* (Minneapolis: Lerner Publications, 1997), 21.

6. David P. Wright, *The Disposal of the Impurity: Elimination Rites in the Bible and in Hittite and Mesopotamian Literature* (Atlanta: Scholars Press, 1987), 15-74.

7. "If someone has a stubborn and rebellious son who will not obey his father and mother, who does not heed them when they discipline him, then his father and his mother shall take hold of him and bring him out to the elders of his town at the gate of that place. They shall say to the elders of his town, 'This son of ours is stubborn and rebellious. He will not obey us. He is a glutton and a drunkard.' Then all the men of the town shall stone him to death" (Deut. 21:18-21).

8. *New York Times*, April 20, 1999.

9. Dante Alighieri, *Inferno*, trans. Stanley Lombardo (Indianapolis: Hackett Publishing, 2009), 331. Dante places Judas in the lowest circle of hell.

10. Toby Keith, "Courtesy of the Red, White, and Blue (The Angry American)," *Unleashed*, compact disc, Dreamworks Nashville, 2002.

Chapter 9

1. Nietzsche, *Twilight of the Idols*, trans. Anthony M. Ludovici (Hertfordshire: Wordsworth, 2007), 5. To be accurate, Kanye's lyrics actually read: "That, that, that which don't kill me, can only make me stronger" (Kanye West, "Stronger," *Graduation*, compact disc, Roc-A-Fella Records, 2007).

2. Bright Eyes, "Waste of Paint," *Lifted, or The Story Is in the Soil, Keep Your Ear to the Ground*, compact disc, Saddle Creek Records, 2002 (emphasis added).

3. Hagner, *Matthew 14–28*, 854. See also John 19:25-27.

4. Ibid. Hagner calls it a "parenthetical note" included by Matthew.

5. *Wikipedia*, s.v. "Mrs. Doubtfire," http://en.wikipedia.org/wiki/Mrs._Doubtfire (accessed March 17, 2011).

6. A January 4, 2008, article on the ABC News Web site referred to painkiller abuse as "America's stealth addiction." It is likely that twice as many people abuse painkillers than cocaine. (See Russell Goldman, "A Fa-

miliar Fiend: Painkiller Addiction," ABCNews.com, January 4, 2008, http://abcnews.go.com/Health/PainManagement/story?id=4082759&page=1.)

Chapter 10

1. Thomas Aquinas, *Summa Theologica* II, I, Question 13: "Therefore if two or more things are available, of which one appears to be more (eligible), it is impossible to choose any of the others" (trans. Fathers of the English Dominican Province [Benziger Bros., 1947], Christian Classics Ethereal Library, http://www.ccel.org/ccel/aquinas/summa.FS_Q13_A6.html).

2. Aristophanes, *Four Plays by Aristophanes: The Birds, The Clouds, The Frogs, Lysistrata* (New York: Meridian, 1994), 525-27. This story is briefly mentioned in William Placher, *Narratives of a Vulnerable God* (Louisville, Ky.: Westminster John Knox, 1994), 4.

3. This verse, for whatever reason, is not included in some of the early ancient manuscripts.

Chapter 11

1. "Church Faces Suit over Boy's Death," *New York Times*, December 19, 1993.

2. "Diabetes Statistics," American Diabetes Association, http://www.diabetes.org/diabetes-statistics.jsp (accessed December 24, 2010).

3. Caroline Fraser, "Suffering Children and the Christian Science Church," *Atlantic*, April 1995.

4. Thao Hua, "Court Upholds Rejection of Suit over Death of Diabetic, 12," *Los Angeles Times*, August 4, 1998.

5. Fraser, "Suffering Children and the Christian Science Church."

6. Søren Kierkegaard, *Fear and Trembling* (New York: Penguin Books, 1985), 81.

7. Ibid., 44-48.

8. "After the two months, she returned to her father and he did to her as he had vowed" (Judg. 11:39, NIV).

9. "O Daughter of Babylon, doomed to destruction, happy is he who repays you for what you have done to us—he who seizes your infants and dashes them against the rocks" (Ps. 137:8-9, NIV).

10. Students of Christian history will be fascinated to learn that the word translated "like" or "similar" here is a version of the word *homoios*, pivotal in the fourth-century debates with Arianism about the nature of Christ. The point is that these commandments are connected, similar but not exactly the same.

Chapter 12

1. Kierkegaard, *Sickness unto Death*, 13-21.

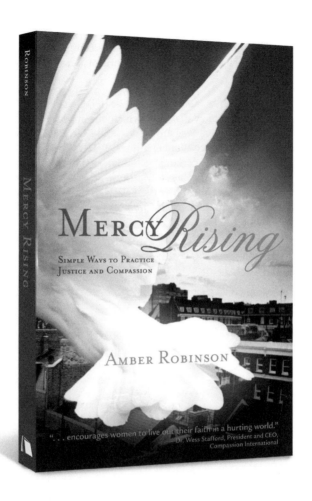